PLAY IT
like you mean it

Supercharge Your Playing
and Let Your Piano Work for You

MagicMusic Productions, Inc.
www.emilepandolfi .com
info@emilepandolfi.com

ISBN: 978-1-7374083-0-7 (print)
ISBN: 978-1-7374083-1-4 (ebook)

Ordering Information:

Special discounts are available on quantity purchases by corporations, associations, and others. For
details, contact sales@emilepandolfi.com

PLAY IT
like you mean it

Supercharge Your Playing
and Let Your Piano Work for You

EMILE PANDOLFI

CONTENTS

PART ONE: ART

PART TWO: APPLICATION PERFORMANCE

CAREER IN MUSIC PART I

CAREER IN MUSIC: PART II
You Have to Have a Judy

Dedication

To pianists everywhere who want to share the music that is in their hearts, and make their music "pop", this book is for you!

It's *"You—only better!"**

**Kevin Nettleingham, friend and recording guru*

PROLOGUE

I sat there, transfixed. The concert hall was by now nearly empty. The cleaning crew were clearing the hall of leftover programs, the occasional errant pair of reading glasses, a handkerchief or two, and other remnants of a great evening at the hall. Alone on the stage, a magnificent Steinway was still breathing hard from the evening's exertions.

The harsh fluorescent work lights began to come on, and the tech crew were closing the lid on the piano, slowly moving its massive bulk side stage to its special climate-controlled cubby on stage left.

Still, I sat there mesmerized, dreaming, longing for more, trying to piece together what had just happened, trying to hold on to an experience that I would carry with me the rest of my life. I didn't want it to end.

And it didn't.

I was eight years old.

A nice lady came and asked me if everything was okay, and where were my parents. I told her that they were there, of course, waiting for me in the lobby. They had allowed me some time with my private thoughts. I just wasn't ready to leave my seat. I asked whether I could sit there a little while longer. "As long as you're okay," she said, not understanding.

What had happened? I had heard a piano played masterfully, certainly! But something much more than that had taken place. I had been transported to a new dimension—not a *place* exactly, but a real, actual different *dimen-*

sion. Why had this particular performance made that kind of impression on me? What had transpired?

It was an evening that had brought forth a mix of tears, intellect, and heart-pounding emotions. I had just heard Arthur Rubinstein play Chopin's Polonaise in A-flat, the encore to a memorable program in the concert hall at the music school where I took my first piano lessons.

At last, shaken out of my trance by the lights and sounds of the mundane world around me, I walked to the lobby in a semidream state, dearly wishing that I could someday create something—even a small part, a shadow—like that which I had just experienced. I wanted to give to others what that artist had given me: an encounter with something outside this universe.

Somehow, we got home. I guess my dad drove us. I sat quietly in the back seat, my parents allowing me the time and quiet to reflect on whatever it was that had absorbed my attention and turned it inwards. I have always appreciated my parents' understanding and respect for experiences that affect me emotionally. That acceptance has stayed with me my whole life and has made me a better artist. I am comfortable with intense emotion.

My parents' gift to me was the gift of appreciation of fine art, and there is no greater gift I could have wanted or received.

That evening I made a covenant with myself. I decided: if you are going to play the piano,

play it like you mean it.

That experience represented a pivotal point in my life and is the one that— 60 years later—motivated me to put my thoughts down in book form.

So who am I, anyway?
"The world's greatest pianist, living or dead!"
(Grandma Pandolfi at her 92nd birthday)

Now that *that's* settled, let's get to what this book is about.

This book is about *you.*

This book found its genesis in my desire to communicate the "how-to" of connecting *emotionally* with the listener. This emotional connection is the true goal of any art form. How you, too, can make that happen is what I hope to share in this book.

You love playing the piano. You probably took some lessons—maybe even for several years—but you don't necessarily play regularly; possibly you are self-taught. Whatever your level, you would like to play more beautifully, more meaningfully, to add elegance and excitement to your interpretations, and to move people (and yourself) emotionally with your playing.

How exactly do you accomplish that? Well, that is what this book is about. It is a *practical* approach to playing more beautifully. Yes, some people are born with an innate ability to reach their audience emotionally. Some of us need a little advice on how to achieve that or how to make our communication with our audience more satisfying or complete. This book is about *everything else* you need to know about playing the piano besides *how to play the piano.* What are those "everything elses" that you need to know? That is what I hope to share.

In each chapter, we will focus on one ingredient of music-making, enough to grab your attention for a time, till you have shifted a paradigm in your thinking. This is not something to *remember* to do; rather, this is an attempt to move you to a new consciousness of your own, where these elements combine to make your playing more beautiful, more engaging, and more satisfying to the listener (according to your own definition). It's how to breathe life into every note you play—how to move the music within the flowing river that it is. It never stands still. It is a dynamic, living creation. You create it newly every time you sit down to play. You should be excited at what you are about to say through your playing.

That said, I am not a pedigreed teacher.

There is no Juilliard on my resumé.

I am first and foremost an empiricist.

Therefore, what I have to offer are those "everything elses" that I have personally discovered along my musical journey over the past 40 years or so.

This book is in two parts.

Part One: Art

Art is all about making your music more exciting and memorable; it's about communicating with intensity on an emotional level. Music has always been a natural second language for me. Somehow, my music resonates with listeners. It always has. When I began this book, it was primarily because I wanted to share what I know about communicating intense emotion at the *piano*. However, the principles discussed apply equally to enhancing your communication of *any kind*, whether it be speaking, dancing, or playing an instrument other than piano. When your music truly connects with people on a personal level, it's possible to become close and intimate with strangers, sharing, in three minutes, a bond more emotionally charged than they typically experience with their close friends. I wanted to let you know how you, too, can make that magical connection happen. In this part of the book, we take a philosophical and holistic view of playing the piano: change your mind, change your playing.

Part Two: Application

There are many people who are excellent musicians, who are considering a career in commercial music but have no idea how to begin. It occurred to me that it could be very helpful for you, the reader, if I were to focus on the business end of making music as well as on the honing of your craft. While I have enjoyed a lifelong education in *classical* music, what I also have to offer is hard-won experience gained over 40 years of a very successful career as an independent musician in the area of *commercial* music—in my case, solo piano arrangements of well-known songs, primarily from movies and musicals. Despite never having had a record deal, I have been fortunate to have sold over 4.5 million albums (before CDs became dinosaurs!), and at the time of writing, my music has been streamed over 750 million times on various platforms.

*Side note: This book is not addressed to the aspiring concert pianist, prepping for international competition—the Olympics of piano playing. There is a path for that noble journey through the great music schools in this country and around the world. Your innate talent and diligence combined with expert mentoring will guide you toward achieving a happy and rewarding life on the concert stage. If you are one of those remarkable people, **put down this book and go practice!***

Neither is this book for those of you who want to make teaching your profession. As I said, I am not a teacher. I am the *product* of many gifted ones. It is because of brilliant, giving people like *you* doing what *you* love that people like *me* can do what *we* love.

So, who's left? Well, for the thousands of musicians who want to make a career in the *performance* of commercial music, whether or not you have had formal training, there is a whole lot to talk about. It is my hope that this book will help you focus your attention more specifically on what it is you think you might like to do for the next 40 years or so and that this part of the book will open your eyes to approaching your creativity from a *practical* viewpoint that you may not yet have explored.

So, let's get to it!

Part One
ART

Chapter 1

MUSIC IS A LANGUAGE

"Musician's voice is music's right to be. And all the rest is merest sophistry."

Why do you play music in the first place?

You play because you feel like it. You have something to say! That's an excellent answer.

Are you playing to enjoy the physical sensation, aural gratification, and expression of emotion through music for *yourself* alone? That is, for many people, a relaxing, invigorating, or meditative pastime that brings them enjoyment and a sense of peace whenever they need it. Sitting at the piano at a stolen moment, or for hours on a weekend, can make you a happier, more fulfilled person, ready to meet the challenges of the coming days. If you are one of these happy people, well then, there are no rules, no parameters; you do what pleases you. Yay for you!

If, however, you want to share with *others* the beauty and excitement you feel when you touch the instrument, why, then you need to know how best to cross that psychological and spiritual divide between you and them. In piano playing, we communicate without the help of words. So, when we say that the piano (or music in general) "speaks" to us, we mean that figuratively *and* literally. The music says what it has to say in a way that we all "get it." Yes, we get it via our own interpretation, but we all know it is meant to be scary or sad or happy. So, we need to know *how* to achieve that.

Early in their education, students spend most of their time mastering the basics, the techniques, developing the muscular coordination, and grasping the theory of the music they are studying *(as they should!).* They become proficient at playing their particular genre of music; in short, they become "good musicians." However, occasionally you find a musician, a concert, a performance that somehow goes way beyond what you have come to believe is great playing, and it is a life-changing experience in that it causes you to rethink some of your deepest convictions about how music should sound and what it should *do* for a listener. Even if you recognize this magic ingredient in others and you believe that you could create that kind of excitement in your own playing, you may feel that you don't know where to start. This book will give you a new look at your technique; it will give you an *understanding* of how to use that technique to connect with your inner beauty, how to put more of yourself into your music, and how to make yourself vulnerable yet unafraid. Therein lies the key to becoming a powerful communicator. Embarking on our philosophical journey from that viewpoint, we discuss how to get that inner beauty across a distance to the listener.

Consider this premise. "One thing cannot be in two places at the same time." But one "non-thing" *can.* This is the essence of the spiritual nature of music, those things we cannot see or touch, but only feel. Music has no *substance* but has tremendous *content.* It is—ironically—a full-to-the-brim, empty vessel, and it can be in two places at the same time: your heart and theirs. That's important. So, let's explore how we can begin this mystical adventure through space and time.

Music is the language that connects one human being to another. Music is, quite literally, a *complete* language, so you need to learn its vocabulary—grammar, punctuation, phrases, pauses, and inflection—just as you would with any other language. Only then can you speak it fluently and get across to people what it is you are actually trying to say. Of course, you have to learn the basics—scales, arpeggios, chords, and phrasing—so that they become second nature. And that is why we spend so much time in the practice room working on those parts of speech.

It is traditional to say that *music* is the international language, but I believe that *emotion* is actually the international language and that music happens to be a wonderful vehicle for conveying that emotion to another person. It bypasses the intellect and goes straight to the soul. Think of music from cultures with which you are not familiar. The music may sound very foreign, or even strange, but the emotional content comes across regardless. If you think of music as a *true* emotional/intellectual language—which it very much is—you can become quite eloquent in its use.

All of the stylistic, melodic, and rhythmic techniques involved in the performance of music are there to support, further, and give life to that end, which is to bring about in the listener a genuine emotional experience.

Even a feeling of deep sadness (when it is presented in an art form—*not in life!*) is very valuable to most people. Sadness in art has a beauty and *deliciousness* to it that we all want to experience somehow. Why do you think *Romeo and Juliet* is considered timeless and universally loved? Surely no one wants to experience that kind of tragedy in real life, but we all savor the emotions that well up inside us as we live vicariously through that story of eternal love.

We all want to experience the feelings of fear or anxiety we find within the pages of a great mystery novel, although we certainly do not want that in our real lives! Great literature and great music can take you to places you have never been, can never or do not want to go. They can make you experience love spanning centuries and can take you on a rollercoaster ride up and down the emotional scale.

Variety and vitality in life and art are qualities that enrich us and broaden our intellectual horizons. You may read Shakespeare and Dickens, but you also might enjoy the more casual, contemporary style of John Grisham. You don't read great books only to enjoy them, or so that you can write in that style, or to "check them off your list"; you read them to *learn* from them, to absorb, to witness all the techniques used, to experience the subtleties, and to savor the nuances of expression penned by the best in a particular field. It's the same with classical music; you want to learn the techniques that lend beauty and excitement, elegance, power, or strength to the sublime outpourings of these great masters. You don't try to imitate them, but their philosophical or technical approach to what they have to say becomes a part of the fabric of your own thinking and becomes part of who you are as a musician.

I notice that many of the qualities people love and admire in the piano playing of classical music—such as inner voice movement, voicing of chords, agogic accents, silences within the music, *rubato*, and the ebb and flow of rhythm—are often absent from the performances of popular music. I believe that *any* style of music played deserves the same loving attention that we, as musicians, traditionally give to the classics.

So, what makes one person's rendition of a piece of music different from that of another? Music is a living, breathing art form. It only exists in real time. It takes three-and-a-half minutes to hear three-and-a-half minutes' worth of music, whereas you can look at a photograph or a painting and grasp its general message within less than a second. With music, you have to be there from beginning to end. But what does that mean for you, the artist? It means that **you** need to be *there* within the music the whole time—living it, moving it, experiencing the swells and decays, being fully *there* in every heartbeat of the music.

I like to compare the playing of a melody to the reciting of a poem or reading of a narrative. Think of a fine actor reading a poem. One of my favorites is Anthony Hopkins reading "He Wishes for the Cloths of Heaven" by William Butler Yeats in the movie *84 Charing Cross Road*. I encourage you to watch it on YouTube and then think of how a less-experienced (or "average") performer would read it. Or listen to David Attenborough narrating the wonderful *Planet Earth* series. Why him? Because he says it like he *means* it. It is not just about getting across the information. The communication must be imbued with *substance*, certainly, but also with the emotional content that hooks your attention and holds it, the *emotional* underscoring that guides you through the *factual* journey—whether it be a spoken narrative or a musical communication—one that has a fulfilling, satisfying conclusion. Yes, music is, quite literally, a complete language.

Often the biggest difference, the greatest divide, between a memorable performance and a "casual" one is this give and take, the ebb and flow of the intensity of the communication. We see all of that in great movie scores because the music is underscoring and supporting the action we are seeing on the screen.

Well, I also think that playing the piano when there is no accompanying action or words needs to be as complete, exciting, and visual an experience as if a movie were playing. In this case, the narrative, the story, and the journey are supplied by the listener; each listener will create his or her own tale by connecting in a real and visceral way with the melody, the power, and emotional content of a strong performance.

We have all experienced getting choked up or having feelings of nostalgia and the reawakening of memories, even physical sensations, when hearing a performance that we personally call "stunning." But we have also experienced the opposite, a technically exceptional performance that comes across as an impressive but somehow unfulfilling show of skill. Yes, music is a language, but *emotion* is the spark that awakens our attention and then engages it throughout the real-time telling of the musical tale. Once you inject emotion into the recounting of a fascinating story, you can then much more successfully

play it like you mean it.

Chapter 2

WHAT IS INFLECTION?

wow...I Mean *WOW!*

What is inflection in music, and why is it worth talking about? The best way to explain what I mean by musical inflection is to compare it to the spoken word. In telling a story, which, as discussed, is what we are doing every time we perform a piece of music, we want to engage our listeners' attention and involvement with the whole story but also to emphasize those parts—a melody, a chord change, an embellishment perhaps—that we find "important." I put the word "important" in quotation marks because what we find important is entirely a matter of judgment and may, in fact, change and evolve over time and as we play the piece. For that matter, it could change *every* time we play the same piece.

I always believe that the piano is trying to say *actual words*. First, you must know what it is you are trying to say. Not a particular storyline specifically, but the general message or direction; perhaps an "I love you!" or "Watch out!" or "This happened in a dream." So, find out what the music suggests to you and then *say* it!

When you are playing a song that *does*, indeed, have lyrics, well, you'd better know them or have them sitting there in front of you while you learn or arrange the piece of music. I love playing music from musicals and some of the great standards because it usually employs wonderful language that tells me what to emphasize when I am in the process of creating a solo piano arrangement of the song. It is the timbre, pace, and modulation of the sound—the *inflection*, far more than actual words—that communicate to another person what is happening in the music.

For example, if you hear shouting in the hotel room next to you, and you can't understand a word of it even when you hold a glass up to the wall (*Oops! Did I say that out loud?*), you can still tell that the people involved are not happy about something. You don't know what, exactly, but you get the gist. The rise and fall of the words spoken tell you a lot.

Likewise, how, for example, can you engage the listener as you recite a poem, or tell a story, without the use of inflection? The absence of inflection comes across as lifelessness, the true definition of "boring." Remember that famous scene in *Ferris Bueller's Day Off* where the high school teacher, played by Ben Stein, is asking the totally uninterested students a question? He and they are completely bored with the subject. He asks for a response in a monotone, slow-paced voice: "Anyone? Anyone?" Even with those simple words, he elevates the feeling of sheer boredom and apathy into an art form through his amazing acting ability. The complete lack of emotion in his voice makes us laugh. Sadly, at the piano, we cannot pull off that little trick. We do not want to be a musical Ben Stein.

Playing music is an art form that needs to develop through the entire duration of the piece you are playing to create its full effect. And during all of that time, you need to hold the listener's interest as he or she experiences the evolution of the music till it blossoms to a satisfying conclusion. Think of it: you are sculpting a figure, painting a scene, right before their eyes (or ears!). It is creation in its nascent state. This is why inflection is so important. Inflection tells you the underlying meaning of a musical phrase as it unfolds. Think of the difference between, say, "I need to buy a *new* car" and "I *need* to buy a new car." The meaning and sense are very different in each case. When you are playing a phrase, think of yourself as an orator. You shape the whole statement as you go. This means **you must know where you are going before you start**. Then you must decide how you will get there. This foreknowledge will lend an elegant logic to your playing. A musical phrase, like a spoken one, is all about inflection.

Some people command attention when they speak. Great speakers may say the same things that other people say, but, for example, when Martin Luther King Jr. says, "I have a dream!" you listen.

When Arthur Rubinstein plays the opening bars of the Chopin Mazurka in A minor, we are moved almost to tears because of the introspective, longing pathos that he puts into every phrase. There are reasons for that. Yes, we can analyze just what he did and what sorts of musical techniques he used, but he is a genius because he used whatever he needed to communicate what he *felt* to anybody who cared to listen. To be moved by Chopin's music may require your *attention* but not a musical *education*. It's not about intellect at that point. The synthesis of a masterpiece of art and a brilliant interpreter creates the magic that we feel when we hear it, just as we feel intense emotion when we hear a great actor recite Shakespeare.

So how do we go about putting inflection into our music? I think of it as sculpting. I use this metaphor because that is exactly what I feel I do when I am playing. How else can you relate the tale that is built into every piece of music—with or without words?

When I am playing a piece of music, I truly want to mold it into to my idea of how I *believe* it should be perceived. Indeed, why else play it? I imagine that the piece of music is pliable, like a piece of clay. And because playing music is a *living* communication unfolding dynamically in present time, you can sculpt it as you go, on the fly—change it, let it evolve, mold it into the finished product you want it to be as you play it.

Isn't that genuinely *remarkable*? It's as if someone were watching you take a lump of clay, and you, with only the magic that lives inside your hands, transform it as they watch, mesmerized, into "a thing of beauty ... a joy forever" (thank you, John Keats). Not only *that*, but "its loveliness **increases!** It will never pass into nothingness" (italics and emphasis added). Read that last part again. "Its loveliness increases; it will never pass into nothingness," said Keats.

Seriously! Isn't it a wonderful feat of legerdemain that one can conjure up intense feelings out of an ethereal nothingness that will then take shape and make their way across the universe into the consciousness of another soul we have never met? Oh my! Oh my! We artists are fortunate *indeed* to be able to take a few choice notes, through the ephemeral medium of sound that doesn't even have physical substance, and turn them into a piece of enduring art that survives long after we are gone! It continues in legacy as an emotional, aesthetic, sometimes *visceral* experience, a poignant memory or a gentle recollection, or perhaps a melancholy reminiscence of times long past. Once we have released it into the universe, it no longer belongs to us but is our gift to the world from then on, going forward, as long as it survives in someone's consciousness.

The Importance of Being Earnest!

When you read that previous paragraph, did you hear it in your mind as a series of disconnected words, thoughts, or ideas? Or did you hear the words resonate in your own mind? And did you incorporate your *own* emotional ebbs and flows into its rhythm, its timing and flow? No two people will read that paragraph at exactly the same pace or with precisely the same interpretation. In other words, did you infuse it with something of *yourself?* Did you imbue those words with life, a life that *you*, the reader, gave them, perhaps with a different shade or emotional tone from that of the author's expression, so as to make that text (a mere series of words and phrases) become more meaningful to you according to your personal story, history, or cultural background? My guess is that you did. How did you do that? With *inflection*, of course. You did it, either unconsciously or purposefully, by following the direction created by the punctuation marks and other grammatical directions, which, of course, is what syntax is for.

For example, in what ways do you say "Good morning" to a baby? Or a puppy? Or a parent? Your grandmother, your best friend, someone you are attracted to, an older person, a total stranger, or your sister or brother? You speak to each of them from a different mindset, don't you? Your voice and delivery sound different to each.

In some of the paragraphs above, I have employed many punctuation techniques: text in **bold**, *italics*, ***italicized bold***, with dashes and parentheses, in addition to more traditional punctuation marks, to make a point and to emphasize words, phrases, or thoughts to which I wanted to draw your *especial* attention.

Speech writers, actors, and script writers do this all the time. I am sure you have done the same with books you read when you highlight or underscore bits of the text that you want to remember. *I* certainly do that with my own scripts of the monologues that I use in my shows to introduce the next song or piece of music that I am about to play. I insert long blank spaces on the page to remind myself to pause before the next important word or perhaps write one or more words in a huge font.

It has less to do with grammatical correctness when you are writing down words to be delivered out loud. You need clues as to how to spread them out, how to give them vitality and substance. It is about energizing an otherwise lifeless text through the power of visible inflection.

Thus, within the music you are playing, the bold, the italics, the long silences, and the huge fonts become *sforzandos*, accents, fermatas, *fortissimos*, *crescendos*, tempo markings, and an overarching feeling of *rubato*, which is a "give and take," rhythmically. It is the interplay, technically speaking, of all these musical directions that lends breadth and scope to the musical utterance. However, these techniques, when they are incorporated over time into the general lexicon of musical performance, are no more considered individual ingredients any more than one thinks of a comma when one is having a live conversation. They have become part of the artist's own musical vocabulary, and they have morphed into what I am calling in this chapter "inflection." It is my hope that this discussion about inflection will help you to

play it like you mean it.

Chapter 3

EMOTION VS. "EMOTING"

I'm an Artist...I'm Sensitive as...as...I'm, Like, *Really* Sensitive!

We have said that playing piano (or making music with any instrument or voice) is all about getting an emotion across a distance to another soul. So, what is the difference between *emotion* and *emoting*?

Julie was a fine pianist—as a matter of fact, one of the finest students I went to school with. She played with passion, correctness, and intelligence. Her technique was excellent. Her hands, arms, torso, and facial expressions of what looked like anguish were a testament to her immersion in the music. She impressed a lot of nonmusicians with her over-the-top histrionics. Yet, while the music she was making was captivating, *watching* her play wasn't. I had to close my eyes in order to see if she had anything to say musically—which she *did!*

So, what is wrong with expressing things through body language when you feel deeply what you are playing? Nothing. But I can tell you what the issue is very succinctly: **sincerity**. In her case, Julie's body motions did not come across as sincere. I am very sure that she *thought* she was being sincere. Perhaps she had seen one of her heroes make those exaggerated motions while playing divinely, and she put that into her mental package of what made that performer so very moving. But without a physical or mental reason for these wild motions, they become at best a distraction and at worst, annoying. In any case, these overdone arm and hand motions (graceful or not) only succeed, whether the performer realizes it or not, *in drawing attention to herself* and diverting it away from the music—the complete opposite (in my estimation) of what you actually want to be doing.

*Side note: Now is a good time to talk about a HUGE exception to this rule, and that is called **show business**. It is not exactly "emoting" but more "choreographed entertainment." I am completely in favor of show business when it is called for. In Los Angeles, I was fortunate to play Gershwin's* Rhapsody in Blue *(along with 83 other pianists) during the opening ceremonies of the 1984 Olympics (hence the 84 pianists in total). It was a **show**! And all of us had choreographed, exaggerated hand and arm movements to do in unison to heighten the look and feel of the spectacular show. These gestures had to be larger than life since we were playing in a massive space, the Los Angeles Memorial Coliseum, for 80,000 people. Likewise, we have all seen beautifully choreographed string ensembles, performers who are elegant in their movements onstage while they play beautifully. It is wonderful to watch! It is true entertainment. That is why it is called show business!*

But I am speaking about a pianist who was trying to *show* us that she felt deeply about what she really may or may not have felt at all. Some people even fool themselves into believing that they are feeling the music in that way when, in fact, they are just drawing all the attention to themselves. It is rather like an actor pretending to cry to *show* us how sad he is instead of really experiencing the sadness that he is portraying. We can all spot bad acting, whether we are educated in that discipline or not.

Conclusion: **remember that it is always all about the music**. If the music, as you are playing, compels you to move one way or another or if the emotion within it makes deep feelings well up from inside and express themselves through your motions, that is fine; that is real. You may not even be aware that it is happening, just as when you tell an exciting story to a friend you are often not aware of how your face looks and how your hands and body move with the tale you are relating. That is real; that is sincere. That is what we want. What I am hoping the student will do is not think that these histrionics are a substitute for genuine emotion. Don't play it like you think it looks impressive.

Play it like you mean it.

Chapter 4

TECHNIQUE

How to Play Like Rachmaninoff in Only 700 Impossibly Difficult Lessons!

(Hint: The First 40 Years Are the Hardest)

With that bit of encouragement, let's turn our attention to an overview of pianistic technique.

Ok, so we are not all technical wizards or child prodigies! (Well, in my case, by the time I was 27 years old, *I* was a child prodigy! So there!) But along our path to becoming better artists, we should all strive to acquire as much technique as we can.

Many years ago, when I was working at a piano bar, during one particularly slow evening I was performing my usual routine of playing whatever tune came to mind, talking with guests, enjoying the evening as I always did, and chitchatting about this and that. After a few minutes, I noticed that a young man was standing behind me, looking over my shoulder, watching intently while I played three or four songs. It was not unusual for people to stand around the piano, come over to the bench, and maybe start a conversation, even while I was in the middle of a tune.

I finished the song I was playing, and this man put his hand on my shoulder. I looked up at him, and he was almost teary-eyed. He squeezed my shoulder and said, very intensely, very sincerely, very quietly, with longing in his voice, "I bet I could do that *if I just knew how.*"

I put my hand on his and said, "I bet you could." In a small way, what he said broke my heart. Here was an artist who knew he could create something of great beauty in his head and heart but—for whatever reason—had never learned *how* to. I knew exactly what he meant.

In order to create great art, you have to know *how to*.

I never saw him again, but I will always remember that profoundly personal exchange.

The art of technique:
In truth, one cannot educate
with only principles concerned
with ideas in their nascent state
but must aspire to impart
the means to *use* the knowledge learned
to turn our ***technique*** into ***art***.

We have all heard our teachers say from the outset that "technique exists to support the music." That is absolutely true and is my view as well. Technique, at its best, is *invisible*. ("He makes it look so easy!")

Technique exists so that the free flow of your musical vision can express itself unimpeded at the piano. Unfortunately, you can't go out and buy it. But if it were available at the local technique store, I would urge you to save all your money and go out and get as big a supply as you could manage. It's usually on sale from when you are around the age of five to around the age of 22 or so. So, get it while you can! Before life gets in the way. You can't have too much. Get to the piano every spare minute and do exactly what your teacher says.

Music is nothing but the communication of experiences, the ebb and flow of emotion, the ups and downs that life presents to us. Technique allows us to make those ideas flow seamlessly from one moment to the next.

That said, concentration on technique *alone* can be an impediment to making meaningful music. When I was recording my album of Chopin gems, my producer stopped me after one of my takes and made this observation:

> "I couldn't hear the musical forest for the technical trees."
> *(Lewis Ross, extraordinary classical guitarist and record producer)*

A point well taken. I played it more musically after that comment.

*Side note: Wonderful exceptions to this rule of course exist when you are discussing a piece of music that is **all about technique**, like the Cziffra octave arrangement of "Flight of the Bumblebee" that takes technique to a stellar level unknown to most of us mere mortals. It's great fun to watch and far more amazing! stupefying! than musically satisfying. It's meant to be. For pure enjoyment and jaw-dropping amazement, watch Yuja Wang play this piece on YouTube.*

So, yes, acquire as much technique as you can in your formative years and then use it wisely. That said, you can always start playing more beautifully from wherever you are, technically. What we are trying to develop here is an elegant shift, *laterally*, in your approach to practice, a subtle adjustment of viewpoint regarding what makes for beautiful communication. Throughout this book, I want you to explore developing your *musical technique* by *changing your mind*—sometimes the hardest thing to do. But we can accomplish that mental shift by examining the thought processes that *precede* the physical movements that the hands and arms make as we play. You are giving musical and philosophical guidance to your hands, which are then doing your bidding. That said, you will find that your finger, wrist, and arm techniques are likely to alter—maybe subtly, sometimes dramatically—because all genuine improvement in any field involving a high degree of skill stems from the attainment of a new level of understanding, which then proceeds into a new *physical* response.

Every time you make a mental adjustment, you will approach your practice of technique in a new way. Scales and arpeggios will not be just a necessary exercise in finger-wiggling; you will begin to view them as a thing of beauty and play them with the same care that you play any musical phrase. Use dynamics, voicing, different touches, shaping phrases—all the ingredients that contribute to a polished performance of an actual piece of music. Love them for what they are giving to your future playing. Just as with the spoken word, the greater your vocabulary, the more precisely you can say what it is you want to say.

To communicate *feelingly* to a listener that which is on your mind or— more to the point—in your heart, you must *own* your technique. Technique must be a plaything, an afterthought, a toolbox that you reach into almost without thinking and take whatever you need from it to get the job done. It should not be noticed by you except as it pertains to the achievement of a more beautiful melody or harmony, or the "bones" of what you are playing. You don't say to yourself, "I will now use my very best *legato* touch to get across a feeling of languor." You just **do it**. The end product of technique is actually "no technique." You *think* it; the hands *do* it. To get to that place, you must have a basic level of physically learned technique at the ready, and the hours behind you spent learning it will have resulted in an ability to *use* that technique to deliver every nuance that you wish to convey into each phrase. It is like a stream of consciousness expressing itself through your fingers.

Why am I going on about this? Well, when one is trying to achieve a **paradigm shift**, one needs to approach it from as many directions as possible. So, pardon me if I sound redundant. It is like breaking a habit; if one is trying to diet or to stop smoking by, say, will power, changing one's routine, or taking temptation out of the way, it takes a great deal of effort and really tests one's mettle—a profound trial of self-discipline.

If, on the other hand, one *sincerely* changes one's mindset, really *gets* what one is trying to do, and finally has that "aha" moment, well then, everything proceeds in a different direction from that moment of paradigm shift forward.

For example, I smoked cigarettes for about 25 years. Then one day, I quit. I am not bragging. Many people do this. I did not accomplish this through the exercise of tremendous self-discipline. I was able to **change my mind** because I decided that it was more aesthetic to *not* smoke. That was my "aha" moment. From that very day on, my new mindset was "Why would I want a cigarette? It's not pretty." All those years before, I had developed a mindset that told me it was more aesthetic *to* smoke because all the "cool" people—actors, models, life-in-the-fast-lane people—were doing it.

So, on to your technique at the piano. Yes, at the beginning, *of course*, practice technique for itself, for the athleticism it brings to your appendages, and for the incomparable feeling of elation that you get from the visceral sensation of pushing the keys. I still do that today.

But there later comes a time when you have to put technique in and of itself aside and make it bow to your whims and fancies. Only when you keep that goal firmly in your mind—*because you believe it!*—as you practice your scales will the practice of technique become an exercise of beauty and joy and not one of drudgery. Each scale, each arpeggio, each broken chord will take you a step closer to being able to

play it like you mean it.

Chapter 5

MELODY

Elvis Is Not King: *Melody* Is King!

I remember as a child practicing the piano while my mother was washing the dishes. No matter what she was doing, she was *always* listening—and offering unsolicited advice. Here is pretty much a direct quote from my mom, a shouted admonition from the kitchen: "***I need to hear the melody! If I can't hear the melody, what's the point?***"

So, I learned early on that all the embellishments in the world are useless if you lose sight (or sound) of the melody. Believe me, that has been the one premise that has guided me in my piano arrangements throughout my artistic career. You can use plenty of pretty musical decorations, as long as you keep in mind that they are there only to support the melody and to convey the meaning of the song. If they don't contribute to that, then out they go.

It mattered not what I might be playing—classical or otherwise—my mother knew that the melody was what the music was all about. If I got too fancy-schmancy with my arpeggios, embellishments, heavy left hand, and so on, she wouldn't have it. It is important to mention here that she herself was not a trained musician, but she *was* a sophisticated listener and a true lover of music and, therefore, my **audience.** (Almost all the time, we musicians are playing for people who are not themselves schooled musicians.)

I often think of that principle as a metaphor for life in general: never lose sight of the melody—that is what it is all about.

"I Just Can't Wait to Be King"

This may seem fairly obvious, but you might be surprised to see (or hear) how many otherwise skillful players don't consistently bring out a melody. I am now referring to ballads, of course, where the song or classical piece is all about the melody. Bringing out the melody is easy, but many people don't do it. Here is why: the person playing the piece, the song, *knows* the melody and is hearing it as he plays. So, he doesn't necessarily consider that he needs to "showcase" the melody (relying, of course, on good taste and training so that he does not overdo it).

What you must take into consideration is that the audience is being introduced to the melody, maybe for the very first time, and therefore needs to be told exactly what the melody *is*, in order to have something to hold on to. You may be surprised to learn that—often—the melody should be played *significantly* louder than the accompaniment. You might, for example, be accustomed to playing a melody at a *mezzo forte* level and the accompaniment at just under *mezzo forte*, not quite *mezzo piano*. I am suggesting, however, that you can play the melody at, let's say, *mezzo forte* and the accompaniment, *pianissimo*. Yes, with that great a discrepancy. Even in a piece of music that, as a whole song, is played at a rather quiet level, a simple one-line melody can be brought out by playing **mf** over a **pp** accompaniment.

You can find a good example of this in my recording of the song "Adagio" by Lara Fabian, in which the melody is **mf** and the accompaniment **pp** or sometimes even **ppp.** We are not splitting hairs here. It doesn't matter what you call it; it is just whatever is required to make the melody sing out, to soar into our consciousness, to live and breathe, to let us know that, *that* is what is important and that it is that which is the *emotion-carrying* message. The terms *"pp" and "mf"* and so on are nonspecific directions and are just useful to describe *relationships* to each other. For example, a *sforzando* played in an environment of quietude would not be played with the same emphasis as it would be in a *forte* aural surrounding, would it? That would make no sense because a *sfz* is an *emphasis*, not a precise volume.

The same goes for the dynamics between the hands. If I were performing the "Adagio" in a large concert hall or on a smaller instrument, the whole piece would naturally be played louder than would the same arrangement in an intimate setting or on a recording where the microphones are picking up every nuance. It just makes sense; however, it bears remarking upon as a player may think that if he rehearsed a piece at a particular dynamic, he must always play it at that level.

Please notice, as you listen to my arrangement of "Adagio," that the "busier" the left hand gets, the quieter the individual notes become because the more notes you play (for example, in a rolling accompaniment), the "louder" the accompaniment seems. There is a lot going on in the underlying figures, so the overall impression is that it is louder, whereas actually you are just hearing more sound at the same level. However, the melody must always reign supreme.

In that piece, there were two ways I could have gone about working with an increasingly busy left hand: I could either have played the melody *louder* or the accompaniment *softer* (which is what I chose). By the way, these are aesthetic decisions made on the spot during performance and recording. They are constant variables.

So how do you practice bringing out the melody when you think you are already doing it?

Here's how: find a piece of music that you already know by heart or by memory and play the melody (usually with the right hand) *stupidly loud* and the accompaniment (usually with the left hand) *stupidly soft*.

Why do I want you to do this? Because at first you will find it annoying or unlistenable, but after you do this *unpleasant* exercise for a while, you will start to listen differently. You may hear different aspects of the melody you are playing that you never heard before. You will hear where to put emphasis in a phrase and the little nuances that had escaped your most scrupulous attention earlier because you were listening to the entire piece altogether, as one whole. And although *you* already knew what the melody was all about, you may want to sculpt it differently now that you are really hearing it in a new light. It is a very educational exercise. Keep an open mind and see what you discover.

Yes, you could play the melody all by itself—with no accompaniment at all—as an excellent exercise, but I want you to realize instead that you need to find out where the melody lives with respect to the entire piece. Remember, as with everything in this book, these exercises and practices are here to bring you to a new place musically and conceptually—to consciously gain for yourself a new way to look at what it is you are trying to do at the keyboard. Everything we talk about is conspiring to get you to more easily

play it like you mean it.

ARPEGGIOS

Up the Down Staircase

I don't have a whole lot to say about arpeggios because they, like scales, are the bread and butter of basic technique, so to remind you to use arpeggios would be like saying, "Remember to use nouns and verbs." But there are a few things I would like to say about their *wise* use.

We all like playing arpeggios. Understandably—they fall under the hand well. They sound impressive; they cover the whole keyboard, and they can add lushness and interest to an arrangement. Arpeggios can even become the entire character or signature of an arrangement or a major part of one. For an example of that last case, please have a listen to my arrangement of "My Heart Will Go On," particularly the introduction.

They are a wonderful tool. They can be gentle and flowing, dynamic and articulate, or intense and moving, as in a low-end accompanying figure.

The only danger here is overuse. It is tempting, I know, to end each phrase of a lovely melody with a little arpeggiated afterthought. "Too many notes," said Emperor Joseph famously in the movie *Amadeus*. Although that is a—purposely laughable—comment by a musically ignorant listener, we don't want to be guilty of filling up aural space by just adding a few extra arpeggios. It can cause ear fatigue or just plain old fatigue!

So, what are arpeggios for? Well, in my opinion, like anything else you do in an arrangement, they must contribute to the feeling you are trying to establish. One example of that is to make a chord sustain. Even the finest piano, due to its physico-mechanical structure, cannot sustain a note or chord longer than a few seconds—dependent, of course, upon the length of the string and quality of the instrument. The great piano makers have created some instruments that have an extraordinarily long-lasting tone, but that quality still differs from instrument to instrument and varies according to the length of the string played. So an arpeggio, tastefully used, can extend the range of that sound way beyond what simply using the sustain (damper) pedal can do.

In order to do that, we must, as in every technique we use, think about the *musical reason* we have chosen to employ that particular technique. In our basic musical arsenal, we should have arpeggios at the ready any time we need them. That said, please remember that you can arpeggiate *anything*. In your studies you are taught to arpeggiate the fundamental chord structures, the traditional colors (major, minor, diminished and augmented triads and sevenths), but I'd like to point out that you can take *any* series of notes and arpeggiate it. That includes extended harmonies, a random series of, say, three or four notes, a portion of a scale, anything you choose. So don't limit yourself to arpeggiating only traditional chords.

The *color* of an arpeggio can create a feeling by its structure. Again, refer to the opening arpeggios in my arrangement of "My Heart Will Go On." It is in the key of E but starts out in the relative C# minor. Those opening measures begin with a whole note octave C# in the deep bass, underpinning an arpeggio consisting of E-B-E—just those three notes. I purposely left out the fifth (G#) because I wanted to paint the dramatic, expansive, dark sound that an open fifth creates. Also, because it is an open fifth, it is neither major nor minor at this point. (It definitely "feels" minor because of the bass C# but only establishes a color when it arrives at the first notes of the melody in E major.) I continue that three-note arpeggio over a bass line going downward from C# to B to A then back up to C# again before settling on the comfortable E major just before the main theme begins. As in any arrangement, it is an artistic decision—nothing more—but I thought it lent a surreal majesty to the opening bars of that poignant, dark, musical tale. I was trying to paint a picture of the rolling waves slowly rising and falling in the dead of a black, frigid night.

Contrast that with a light, slow-moving *pianissimo* arpeggio that begins in the extreme upper register and *descends*, drop-like (with a staccato touch over the sustain pedal) down, coming to rest in the quiet satisfaction of a closing harmony or a gentle melody. I visualize the fiery cinders drifting downward from a fireworks display. You can find an example of that in my arrangement of "When You Wish Upon a Star" (in the opening bars of the actual tune, right after the introduction).

You see what I am trying to do here: I want you to use your imagination to paint a picture, to create an image of what it is you want to show the listener before you just decide to use an arpeggio. The visual/aural *intent* is what we are trying to get across—not the sequence of notes themselves, the arpeggios, or the crashing chords. We must know what it is we are trying to create—whether, for you, that be aural, or visual, or intellectual—before we decide how to achieve it. The arpeggio is nothing more than another wonderful piece of currency in your musical wallet. Spend it wisely.

And that's all I have to say about that!

Play it like you mean it!

Chapter 7

FINGERING

A Rule of Thumb

The reason there are traditional fingerings for scales, chords, and arpeggios is that over time—hundreds of years, in fact—these fingerings have been found to be the most efficient, logical, or convenient; they fall under the hand most naturally. That said, as you develop your technique, please remember that the physical architecture of hands differs from person to person, and what is relaxed and comfortable for one hand can be difficult—or even painful—for another. The truth is it doesn't matter what finger you use. My overall rule is usually to go with the one that is closest to the spot, the path of least resistance, the easiest way. You want to get to a point where specific fingering is not important. Getting the sound you want *is*.

Don't fall into the habit of believing that some fingerings are strictly taboo. An example of that is "in scale passages you must never put the thumb on a black key." Or, "you must never play a trill with the third and fourth fingers." Most often that is excellent advice. But that pedantic instruction was never intended to be sacrosanct, and yet, what gets impressed into our malleable minds during our fledgling years we often—understandably— take as gospel. The danger with this is that over time, these "rules" begin to harden, to ossify into immutable "laws," and thus interfere with our path to easy technical freedom. In a challenging passage, we may—without realizing it—fail to explore a number of different solutions to a performance problem because we never even *considered* trying a "forbidden" fingering.

There are literally hundreds of these unspoken considerations that creep into our consciousness undetected and can stay with us well into our mature thinking/playing years. I know what I am talking about here. To this day I still occasionally hear the remnant of a tiny inner voice telling me I "shouldn't" use a certain finger on this particular note. I do it anyway, but the fact that I think of it as doing it "anyway" means that I had to discuss it with my inner self and determine that I was going against standard practice, that I was still being a little bit of a rebel. That consideration should not be anywhere in the mix. We want to get rid of an old way of thinking, not by "conquering" it or replacing it with a new approach; rather, we want to embrace a larger picture that *includes* the new way of thinking. This is not a maverick approach to problem-solving but rather an open-minded, comfortable consideration of all options *including* the tried-and-true traditional ones. That is how we move forward. Relevant to *this* chapter, the goal of feeling an easy indifference in considering what finger to use is nothing more than removing mental objections to trying new things. Like everything else in this book, this is about how to free your thinking in general and, in this way, move you into a new realm in your artistic and life expression—one in which you can let your creativity soar through the free flow of musical ideas, unhampered by old, dusty considerations that restrict what you have to say at the instrument, mentally or physically.

Art is life, and life can be an art form. In either case, you have to remove the mental shackles that keep you from embracing new ideas while honoring the old. By taking this holistic view of fingering you have moved another step closer to being able to

play it like you mean it.

Chapter 8

EMBELLISHMENTS

Pass the Cinnamon-Infused Cranberry-Orange Sauce, Please

Let's talk about condiments. Embellishments are just that: they are orna-ments, decorations, touches of color, sparkles, and flights of fancy. They can breathe new life into a musical phrase.

Examples of embellishments are trills, mordents, turns, grace notes, glis-sandos, scale passages, and others. They are usually nonessential notes used to color a main melody line. There are any number of variations, as they are often the extemporaneous additions of a composer (or improvisor) to the melody line he or she is playing and may not happen the same way in the next iteration of that line.

Embellishments should not usually take your attention away from the ac-tual melody; rather they should subtly enhance it. They can occur any-where in the piece because they are a tool, an accoutrement. Think of an outfit that a celebrity is wearing. Do the necklace, earrings, and hair orna-ments draw attention away from the gown, or do they complete the overall look? That is a handy analogy because, if done "wrong," we at once feel that the outfit is in poor taste or doesn't make sense aesthetically.

And speaking of that, when purposely overused for really humorous effect, embellishments can be outlandishly funny. Think of a feather boa, an outrageous fur hat, or some other outré sartorial accoutrement *(affectation intentional!)*.

The same thing can happen in music. In other words, don't overuse. Embellishments are there to emphasize, set the scene, gently highlight a phrase, or draw attention to the actual substance of what is being said, but not to try to take center stage.

That said, embellishments abound in Chopin's music and are quite extraordinarily beautiful in his hands, remembering, of course, that he is Chopin, and we are not. For most of us, ornaments can very quickly become an impediment, rather than a help to the overall musical communication. Don't use ornamentation just for sake of using it. Remind yourself that these melodic decorations are the musical equivalent of condiments and spices to enhance—not take over—the flavor of the entrée. They are not the main course. They usually function as "ear candy," and although initially pleasing, they—like too much sugar—can quickly cloy and leave a saccharine musical taste in our ears.

As far as when and where to employ embellishments, there are no real "rules of usage." But that is incomplete. What we *should* say is "There is one rule with embellishments, as with all the other elements of creating an arrangement: use your musical good judgment and don't make an embellishment meaningless." It must contribute to the whole "feel" of the piece.

That said, those devices that we usually call ornaments, like trills for example, *can* on occasion be the focus of a piece and powerfully engage the listener's attention. Think of the opening bars of "Ritual Fire Dance" by Manuel de Falla. The exciting opening trills set the mood for the whole piece. In that case, the trill is certainly not an embellishment but actually the defining character of the piece.

Always keep in mind what are you trying to say to the listener. If embellishing an idea that you just stated helps get the emotional goal across, then by all means, use it to help you to

play it like you mean it.

Chapter 9

SUSTAINING NOTES ON A PIANO

Can't You Linger Just a Little Longer?

When you play a note on the piano, you hear the initial attack, and then the note immediately begins to decay. That is the nature of the instrument. So how do we sustain a note or a harmony that we need to make last over a period of time while other (melodic) things are going on?

There are several ways:

1. Trill. You can play a trill with the first and second fingers of, let's say, the right hand, while using the other three fingers to play the melody above that inner trill. This gives the trilled notes a sustain for as long as you keep the trill going. The trill can be a part of the actual melody, extending the melody notes far longer than they would otherwise last. One of the most sublimely elegant examples of a trill being used to "speak" the actual melody can be heard about three-quarters of the way through the first movement of the Ravel Piano Concerto in G.

2. Tremolo. This is like a trill, only the notes are not adjacent. You can hear an absolutely gorgeous example of this technique in the interior

of the cadenza of the first movement of the Grieg Piano Concerto, where the outer fingers play the melody in octaves and the tremolo is played inside with the second and third fingers.

3. Left-hand bass rolling arpeggio. Listen to the opening of my arrangement of "Music of the Night." Here the arpeggiation is not distinct: I hold the sustain pedal down and play the notes gently. I am not bringing any notes out above the others, just making a "wash" of sound, and not worrying about meter or rhythm. I am just creating a backdrop of "D♭-ness" with a slow arpeggio.

4. Echo technique. Play a chord that you want to sustain, hold it with the sustain pedal, and then every so often play it again as gently as possible, so that the hammers just barely "kiss" the strings, and there is almost no audible repetition of the attack. This is rather like the real-life echo of a sound in which, as it fades, the initial attack becomes softer and softer till it finally disappears, and you are just hearing the harmony hang longer in the ear. Whenever I do that, as in the above method, I don't pay any attention to the rhythm or meter; I just keep trying to make the harmony linger. You can also employ this technique with an individual note and create an echo effect. It's really lovely. Have a listen to the opening bars of my arrangement of "Promenade Sentimentale" on my *Quiet Passion* album for a good example of this "echo" technique.

In summary: there is always a way. Use your imagination and don't be bound by the "tried-and-true" methods of achieving your desired sonic result. Think of everything you know about how the piano makes sounds and then delve more deeply into your own creativity. There is boundless fun to be had in this journey of exploration! One more step closer to being able to

play it like you mean it.

Chapter 10

DYNAMICS

Color Your World!

One of the many magnificent attributes of a piano is its inherent dynamic range. As a solo instrument, nothing exceeds the dynamic range of a piano. And that is exciting! We have so great a tool, literally at our fingertips. So, by all means use it! With the twitch of a finger, we can play the loudest *fortissimo* or the smallest *pianissimo* in an instant. That is a wonderful gift!

So, let's talk about how we produce these great variants in volume and why. Dynamics lend interest, emotional content, and excitement to your playing. One of the biggest differences between "background" music and live performances is that in background music, the dynamics are purposely kept at a monochromatic level. The music is meant to *not interfere*. But we are talking here of piano *performance*, where the pianist is engaging the listener in what it is he or she has to say, musically. The ebb and flow of dynamics in a piece of music make it more interesting. Because dynamics affect us viscerally, they add a depth of feeling to any communication.

Let's start with a word about playing extremely loud passages. Don't hurt yourself! *Remember that the volume of a note on the piano is directly depen-*

*dent upon how **fast** the hammer hits the string, not how **hard**.* Once the sound has been produced, you instantly let your fingers and hand relax. It only takes about 50 grams of pressure to keep the key depressed. How much is that? Very little.

A good exercise for playing *fortissimo* would be to play a thick chord (four fingers of each hand), concentrating on the *speed* of moving the hammers against the strings, and then *instantly releasing all pressure (except enough to keep the keys from coming back up)*, being mindful as you do it of how *relaxed* the hand feels. The natural weight of the hand is keeping the keys depressed at that moment. If someone were to come over and quickly lift your wrist up from underneath, it would take no effort at all. Your hand and wrist would feel limp and relaxed. Your hands are doing an ongoing dance between maximum power and limp spaghetti *(al dente, of course! with Bolognese sauce like Mom used to make—dang! And cannoli for dessert. Yum!)* Oops! What were we talking about?

Oh yeah! Playing loud.

You could, of course, also do this drill with one finger at a time. It's a sweet feeling when you think, "Wow! How fast I can move the hammer and instantly relax!" It's actually quite invigorating because you have found out what power you have with very little effort expended. When playing rapidly at volume, this can't happen after each individual note, but overall you will be aware that once you have made a sound, loud or soft, your finger, hand, wrist, and forearm can relax utterly. You are now simply holding a place on the keyboard, ready for the next note(s).

I like to compare this to Bruce Lee's famous "one-inch punch" wherein he could break a board starting within only an inch of the board or knock an opponent backward from only a few inches away from the man's body. How could he do this? By generating such *speed* instantly from a totally at-rest position. A bullet does its damage because of speed, not size or inherent strength. If you threw a bullet at someone, nothing would happen.

So, speed translates into power and muscle, but you must—at least at the piano— think in terms of *motion*, instead of pressure. This will keep you from injuring yourself when playing at high volume over a period of time.

Now, how about playing *pianissimo*? There is a wonderful quotation on this very subject from one of South Carolina's poets laureate, who is also my friend, that, with her permission, I quote here:

> *"It doesn't mean silence, like the absence of the moon in the day sky.*
> *It doesn't mean barely to speak in the way of a child's whisper. To play*
> *Pianissimo is to carry sweet words to a lonely woman in the last row of*
> *a concert venue who cannot hear anything else and to lay them across*
> *her lap like a cape."* (Verna Puntigan, SC Poet Laureate 2011)

Isn't that beautifully said? So, how do we achieve that kind of *pianissimo* that reaches all the way through the hall and feels like a gentle caress? Well, for a start, if we do the opposite of playing *double-forte*, then we would move the hammers toward the strings *very slowly*, right? That is technically true, but there are exceptions. And we must practice moving the key not *so* slowly as to make no sound at all.

I suggest, for *pianissimo* practice, that you start by playing a note one at a time with each finger to just feel the key depth on that particular piano. You should play *without making a sound* at this point, just *feeling* the key: how much effort it takes to move the key, exactly when the hammer approaches the string, but not touching it because the hammer drops back at that point. You can feel the little "bump" in the travel of the hammer. Form an intimate connection with the instrument; get to know what's actually happening.

Go to a piano store and look at an exposed piano action. Or next time your piano tech comes to tune your piano, have him or her take the action out so you can have a look and spend some time watching what happens when you depress a key; or if they are voicing or regulating the instrument, ask lots of questions about what they are doing. Become a pest and find out as much as you can about the subtle workings of the action.

This is useful so that when you next play, you know what is happening inside the instrument. You are not just pushing a key. You are controlling the speed of a highly sophisticated lever where, in a good instrument, a series of events respond to your every musical thought. So, you must make a decision at every moment as to how you wish to move the hammer and therefore control the manner in which the hammer makes contact with the string.

Here is another observation about playing *pianissimo*. As mentioned above, you don't want to play so softly that you are not heard at all (depending on the environment in which you are playing). In a *pianissimo* passage, we still want to make the melody stand out. Experiment with playing the accompaniment as softly as possible and the melody above it, say, *mp*, or even *mf*. You might be surprised to find out that the overall impression on the listener is that the entire passage is very quiet indeed, when in reality you are just making the accompanying figures sound far away in the depth of the texture. You are creating the *illusion* of *pianissimo*, while still bringing to the fore what is most important. In addition, there is something deliciously sweet to the ear about the two disparate dynamics being heard at the same time. That is one of the most beautifully elegant attributes of a piano.

A wonderful example of that dynamic illusion can be heard in the closing bars of "Clair de Lune," where the music dies away as the bass notes progress up the keyboard. The final high treble third (Debussy's marking: "*pp* dying away") must be played at least *mf* in order to be heard for more than a second or two, as it is in such a high register that it will die away very quickly under the rising left-hand arpeggio if you play it *pp*. A hammer can touch a string gently, powerfully, even angrily, depending on *you* and how you feel at that instant. But it will only respond to your touch if you know how to touch it.

Chapter 11

CRESCENDOS AND DIM-*INNUENDOS*

What Are You Implying?

Crescendos

Here's a little discussion about the use of *crescendos*. *Crescendos* can be truly exciting! Invigorating! Thrilling, even! Or satisfyingly slow and smooth. They impart another dimension to the music you are playing. They can be short and to the point or can last through a whole piece of music. Occasionally in a classical piece, these dynamics are a focal point of the whole musical journey.

The most notable example of that last case, is, as everyone knows, Ravel's *Boléro*, in which the snare drum starts out *pianissimo* and grows throughout the piece to a glorious *fortissimo* at the end. It's quite a feat for the percussionist and quite a remarkable experience for the listener. That's what the piece is all about: one long, huge, satisfying *crescendo*. A dramatic enough ingredient that you cannot tear yourself away; you *need* to hear the whole thing!

Most *crescendos*, however, last only a few notes or a few bars, and are used mainly for color and character, just as they would be in the reciting of a story by a skilled orator. In fact, as I have mentioned before, most pieces of music are, indeed, telling a story. The dramatic or subtle changes in volume give a direction and purpose to what the music is about. So, the use of *crescendos* is one of the many tools that one has at one's disposal when playing a musical phrase. Don't think of a *crescendo* as simply "getting louder," rather think of a *crescendo* or *diminuendo* as inflection, which it truly is. These devices can hold the listener's attention throughout a phrase or a whole piece of music.

Like any other expressive ingredient in the performance of music, there is more than one kind of *crescendo*. Depending on the nature of the whole piece, a *crescendo* can increase in volume very evenly and smoothly or can have a gentle beginning and then snowball toward the end, concluding in a thrilling climax of sound. I believe *(and this is entirely a judgment call)* that you sometimes need to make your emotional expression larger than life in order to get your musical point across. (See Chapter 14, "Bang Out the Subtleties!") Experiment in building a *crescendo* by small increments at first and then really ramp it up toward the end. This can be electrifying!

When playing a *crescendo*, be very sure you know at what dynamic level you intend to end and how long it will take to get to the top of the *crescendo*. Go over that in your practice. Try a dozen different ways of increasing the volume. Write notes to yourself on the page, reminding yourself where you are in the progression of the *crescendo*. Make it satisfying. It's like a lot of other things in life, not just figuratively, but literally. You just know when the move from soft to loud (or the reverse) is "right."

The lesson here is that all changes in volume are not created equal, and you can play with the rate of change. Think of a *mezzo forte* passage moving up little by little, almost imperceptibly, *getting louder* and then, as the individual notes progress toward the climax of the phrase, snowballing—*getting much bigger, much faster*—into a thrilling conclusion! This sort of treatment of a *crescendo* creates an excitement, a momentum, an unstoppable juggernaut of sound that captures the listener's attention and leaves her eagerly anticipating the exciting, satisfying conclusion of this musical statement. She cannot take her attention away. It is a compelling story—even if only for a few bars—that one *must* listen to till the end.

There is another type of *crescendo* that I would like to touch upon. It is not *technically* a *crescendo* per se, in that one doesn't actually increase the dynamic. Rather you achieve a "bigger" sound by thickening up the texture. Rachmaninoff does this beautifully in both the "18th Variation" (from *Rhapsody on a Theme of Paganini*) and in the Prelude in C# Minor, where each iteration of the melody contains fuller chords, with more notes in each chord so that the overall sound is that much larger. Yes, you can also play a traditional *crescendo* at the same time, but even without that, you are giving the illusion of volume increase through a saturation in tone. It is very much like a solo violin playing a passage at a soft level (*pp*) and then having the entire string section of the orchestra play the same passage at the same dynamic level (*pp*). It's a richer, fuller, more sonorous sound and can add aural interest to your arrangement of a song. In my piano solo arrangements, I often use both techniques, an increase in volume *and* a thickening in texture.

Diminuendos

Well now, what shall we say about *diminuendos,* the other side of the dynamics coin? Just the reverse, of course. You can play with *diminuendos* the same way that you do with *crescendos,* making the dynamic change smoothly, with a snowball effect, or the thinning of the texture, and with a long or short duration.

Diminuendos can also give the feeling of moving out of a real-life setting into a dreamlike state. This can be illustrated when a sound dies away at the end of a piece, like the closing motif of the Mazurka in A Minor, op. 17, no. 4 by Chopin, where the final motif doesn't *end* exactly; it mimics the opening bars of the piece and drifts off into another dimension. As a listener, you can still hear the notes in your memory after they have stopped sounding. It invites you to continue the sound painting; it's like watching a cloud slowly dissolve. When did it finally disappear? These are all feelings, ideas to ruminate on. Again, these are my interpretations of various aspects of sound. I truly believe that, as a performer, you must make these images very real to yourself in order to get them across to the listener.

This does not mean that the audience will see what *you* see; but they will feel the emotional content that comes across through the magic that is music, but only provided that *you* feel and see it. I am not sure how this happens, but it does. Music transfers a vibrational dimension that resonates with another soul. It just happens. That has been known for centuries, and it is as remarkable and mysterious today as it was all those centuries ago. Pretty wonderful. *Crescendos* and *diminuendos* are two more tools in your bag of tricks to help you weave that magic spell. Remember, you are giving the listener a gift of an emotional experience. That is what this book is all about. Don't hold back.

Play it like you mean it.

Chapter 12

ACCENTS

"You've Got to Ac-*cen'*-tu-ate the Positive!"

Accents in music, as in speech, are a powerful tool and can be used to communicate to the listener the most important or meaningful sounds within a musical texture. There are numerous ways to accentuate a particular element of a piece of music, just as there are in speech. Those expressions live in the hands of the creator of the music or the teller of the story. There are three main kinds of accents that I would like to address here: **dynamic** accents, **harmonic** accents, and **agogic** accents. Let's discuss each separately.

The most frequently used is the **dynamic** accent. That, of course, is the drawing of attention to a note or chord by simply playing it *louder*! Ironically, you can achieve a very similar and exciting effect by playing it suddenly much *softer* as well (*subito piano*).

The important thing to remember about a dynamic accent is that it can occur anywhere within a piece of music: it can be used to emphasize an inner voice or to bring out one note within a chord (as in chord voicing) or in any part of a phrase, not just the (most obvious) beginning or end. Can you see what a wealth of interest you can generate within your music with the judicious use of accents? As with all of these musical techniques, these elements lend added life to your playing, which is exactly what we are trying to accomplish here: making your music something worth listening to. To hold someone's attention, you need to engage their interest in a genuine way. You don't *demand* that they listen, or hope they like it, or do musical "tricks" to get their attention; you actually invite the listener to enjoy what you are doing by creating interesting sounds for them to listen to, to engage with, *n'est-ce pas?* Dynamic accents can be gentle or heavy-handed. An accent mark noted within a *pianissimo* passage is, obviously, to be played much less loudly than one in a *forte* phrase. Dynamic accents, as with all three kinds of accents, don't have to **shout!**

So, on to the **harmonic** accent. This is a more subtle type of accent, by which I mean you don't *necessarily* play these notes any louder or softer than their neighbors. Rather, you want to bring attention to a change in harmony, perhaps a change from minor to major (often used), which opens up the music and makes you (metaphorically) sit taller, feel uplifted, and open your eyes a little wider as you listen.

The converse is also true. You can induce a furrowed brow or a change in temperament by simply moving abruptly from a bright harmony into a dark one, usually from major to minor. Even a subtle change in harmony—*laterally*, as it were—can raise an eyebrow or bring a feeling of anxiety. Think of scary music in a movie score. The sudden harmonic change lets us know that something dark is about to happen—even *before* the actual action happens in the film. It's not necessarily louder or softer, just a change in color. This can happen when a consonant harmony changes into a purposely "out-of-tune" one or the reverse, where a discordant sound finally resolves into a comforting sonic embrace. All of this can happen in a moment somewhere within the entirety of a piece of music, yet it will remain in the listener's consciousness after the music has died away because it infuses a sense of drama into the musical context and offers a welcome relief when it finally resolves. In our own playing of a piece of music, whether it be a classical piece or an arrangement of our own creation, we are giving the listener something to commit his emotional attention to at that moment.

Similarly, we all know the exhilarating sensation we feel when a piece of music modulates to a new, higher key, often just one half step or whole step up. It is this harmonic change that makes our ears (and hearts) perk up when it happens. Composers use this technique when they want to give the music a new sense of "one more time, with feeling!" in the last run through the hook of a song, for example. In the realm of pop music, have a listen to "Perfect Illusion" by Lady Gaga for a great example of a key change that pumps new life to an already exciting song.

In other words, harmonic colors have the power to elicit a variety of emotions in people. They are a powerful tool in the collection of musical resources that are—literally—at your fingertips.

The third kind of accent is one of the most exquisitely elegant and sophisticated gems in our musical repertoire: the **agogic** accent. It is an accent of *duration*, rather than volume or pitch change. Agogic accents impart a kind of nobility to a phrase. I can best describe the effect of an agogic accent as that of watching a drop of water clinging to the underside of a leaf, giving itself over to the delicious lure of gravity, gaining enough weight, momentum—*desire*, even!—to *finally* drip down onto the water below. The effect is an exhilarating one of anticipation and then relief as the water droplet (or the note) relaxes, resolves, and disappears into its satisfying reunion with the body of water (or musical tapestry) of which it is but a tiny part.

As with all musical elements, these three types of accents should be regarded as sculpting tools with which you mold your musical clay and not as technical "tricks." Much of what we are talking about here you probably already do intuitively, just as you ordinarily speak with inflection. But it is worth focusing your attention on, as the more intently you examine the elements of your playing, the more ideas will come to you, all with a common goal: to

play it like you mean it.

Chapter 13

CHORD VOICING

The Voice above the Crowd

Chords are, in a sense, the *body* of the music you are playing; by which I mean they are the warp and woof of the tapestry, the canvas, if you will, onto which the melody, rhythm, motion, and direction of the music are painted. Chords are, to me, *visceral*, in that they are tactile, satisfying to feel under the hand, and they are the foundation upon which the piece of music is built. You can almost "taste" chords.

Chords can be played as a backdrop, monochromatically, or they can be extremely colorful; the latter is what I would like to discuss here.

Anytime you play a chord, you must decide which note (or notes) of the chord is to be the most crucial to the direction of the music you are playing, according to your musical taste. **"Voicing"** a chord means bringing out one or more notes of the chord so as to give those notes more significance than their neighbors. How is this accomplished?

Well, technically, here is what is happening: If you keep in mind that *the volume of a note played on a keyboard is dependent upon how **fast** the hammer hits the string,* the note you want to feature needs to move faster than the other notes of the chord. Yet all the hammers need to "land" (hit the strings) at the exact same time. Logically, therefore, the emphasized note has to be struck an instant later and an instant faster than the surrounding notes, right? Right. Seems difficult, yes? Well, technically it *is* complex, and if you try to analyze it and do what I just described, it *is* difficult. However, in actual practice, it can be accomplished reasonably quickly with the two following exercises.

1. **First Method: Finger Flickin' Good!**

    Let's say you are playing a C-major triad (with the octave C) with your right-hand fingers (1, 2, 3, 5), and you wish to bring out the upper C. Start to press the C, E, and G, and at the last moment before they hit the key bed, "flick" your pinky finger (5) so that it hits bottom at the same instant as the other notes. Do this about a hundred times or so till you get the hang of it. Now try emphasizing the low note C. Do it over and over until you stop thinking about it and just try to "get" it. You will find that after a while, the finger in question "flicks" itself at the last moment. Practice this in turn with each of the notes in the chord. Any chord. Both hands.

    At first it may be more difficult to bring out the *inner* chord values, but that, too, is mostly a psychological issue, not a physical one. You will likely make the error, at first, of pushing harder with one finger. The truth is all you have to do is *hear* the note you wish to emphasize. After a while the muscles of your hand and arm will adjust themselves. Easier said than done, I know, but this technique will lend a new dimension of interest to the listener. Yes, it really will become second nature after a while, and yes, it really does matter.

2. **Second Method: Flammit!**

    This is a technique borrowed from percussionists. The way that you play a **flam** on a snare drum, say, is that you start with one stick higher than the other and move them downward—at the same speed—so that the closer stick hits the drumhead first, followed immediately by the second stick. The result is that of a grace note with a primary note, together called a "flam."

OK, so if we alter this technique to suit our purposes, *which is to have both notes sound at the same time but with one note louder,* we start the same way: The finger we wish to emphasize is raised—ever so slightly—higher than the other fingers. In most piano technique, the fingers are already touching the keys before we play a note, but in this exercise, only the finger that is going to be emphasized is slightly *above* the key. Then we move all the fingers downward with the intention of all of them hitting the key bed at the same moment, so the raised finger has to (automatically) move a tiny bit faster than the others in order to hit bottom at the same time and thus sound louder. Again, at first it is a mental-physical conundrum of sorts, but you will get past that rather rapidly as you listen, listen, listen!

Now, these methods sound pretty complex and difficult to master. *And they are!* But I believe there is a much easier way to achieve the same results. I have used this method for years. This is the **"think method"** *(that term, of course, borrowed facetiously from* The Music Man. *Hah! I knew there was some substance to Professor Harold Hill's band teaching method!)*

3. **Professor Harold Hill's Method**

So, you start by practicing the methods above, paying close attention to the note you want to feature. Just play the same chord over and over, listening very intently to what you are playing, *wanting* to hear that one note, *insisting* upon hearing that one note, *willing* it to speak, *knowing* that, that one note standing out will make that chord more beautiful, more meaningful, and more satisfying in the context of the music you (will be) playing. At first you may have some weird things happen with the muscles of your hand till you wrap your wits around the concept. However, your thoughtful persistence will reward you with results.

Eventually—and I mean this literally—*all you will have to do is hear the note you wish to emphasize, and your hand will do your bidding.* After a while, the muscles of the shoulder, arm, hand, and fingers will readjust themselves. They will know what to do. It sounds hard to believe, I know, but it will happen. Guaranteed! And this technique will lend a new dimension to your playing.

This may seem a little like magic or daydreaming, so let's look at an example of something we all do every day, like catching a falling object. Think of it. In a split second, the physical and mental processes within the body have to align to produce the exact chain of microactions needed to catch the china cup before it hits the floor. How much pressure does your hand put around the falling object as it is caught so as not to break it? What if you are catching a wooden bowl or a dish towel? Every object is different, yet we react with astounding precision. If a biologist were to explain the concatenation of events necessary to achieve such coordination, I am sure it would take pages of very detailed explanations that would lull most of us into a glazed-eyed stupor. I can only guess that these are the kinds of challenges that robotics builders face every day. How many different decisions, estimations of effort, pressure, distance, speed, and numerous other split-second calculations need to be made to culminate in a simple physical motion that moves speedily and without error to its goal?

Yet we humans do it—unthinkingly—all the time. But how is this even possible when it comes to catching the cup? Well, you can do it because your instantaneous mental directive supplied everything—*the only thing!*—the mind-body needed to set itself to the successful accomplishment of your thought-of goal: your instantaneous decision to catch the falling object.

For the same mind-body that controls your breathing, monitors your heart rate, and manages innumerable complex systems without any contribution by your conscious self, this catch-the-object-before-it-hits-the-floor task is the simplest of simplicity. After a while, all you do is ***intend*** for an action to take place. There is no thinking involved anymore.

This is not muscle memory; it is far better in that it is the brain-body alliance making the myriad decisions necessary to accomplish this amazingly complex objective that you have silently set it to do. In the twinkling of an eye.

It's exactly the same with the voicing of chords. You hear it in your mind; you intend it, and the body does it. Thank you, Professor Hill.

I hope this helps. It will dress your chords in sartorial finery, aurally speaking. This is one more ingredient to help you

play it like you mean it.

Chapter 14

NUANCES

Bang Out the Subtleties!

I would like to comment on some of the understated components of your music, such as inner voice leadings, bass-line motion, delicate interior changes in harmonies, and gentle things like that. And here it is, in a nutshell:

bang out the subtleties!

I am, of course, being facetious. But I do want to make a point; **don't be so subtle that no one can hear you.** But at the same time, don't be crass. Don't overdo it. Like so many things, it's a judgment call.

When you want to draw attention to a subordinate event in a piece of music, you need to do just that; *draw attention to it*. By this, I mean, you may have to *emphasize* the secondary voice you wish to feature a bit more than seems natural to you. Why is that? Well, *you* are performing the piece; you know it inside and out, all its secrets. You can hear the inner workings of the music since you put them there. You will hear every note you play. But this is not a given for your first-time listener.

Sometimes when I am playing, I notice that I have selective hearing. I hear what I *want* to hear, which is not necessarily what the listener is hearing. The listener's ear is going to be focused on the main event, i.e., the *melody*, in most cases. So, if you want them to hear an elegant subtlety within the fabric of the music, you need to direct their attention to it one way or another, whether it be with a slight increase in volume or a delicate change in tempo or texture. You have to point it out. Think of being guided through an art museum by a knowledgeable curator. She will uncover mysteries within a painting that you would otherwise have missed completely.

It is not the audience's responsibility to detect all the nuances you have spent so much time engineering into your performance. Their attention should be (gently) guided to the intangible ingredients of your playing that lend color and interest to your overall rendition of the piece.

Give that some thought. Don't squander the opportunity to infuse a bit more magic into your playing. Giving careful attention to these subtleties in your performance will make you better able to

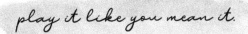

play it like you mean it.

Chapter 15

PEDALING

Put the Pedal to the Metal!

Wow! One of my favorite topics! We will discuss the usage of all three pedals on the piano, but let's begin with the sustain pedal because it is the one most often used, even by beginner students.

I'm Pedaling as Fast as I Can!

The sustain pedal (actually the *damper* pedal because it lifts all of the dampers at once when you depress it) is one of the most useful mechanical/musical contrivances ever invented! There is so much you can do with it besides sustain a note or chord.

The first thing we are taught to do with the sustain pedal is to let the pedal up *(which means the dampers down)* cleanly every time the harmony changes. That is a very good rule and one that should be adhered to most of the time. The sustain pedal can assist (but not take the place of) true *legato* when the notes to be connected are out of reach. But it must be done cleanly. Sloppy or indifferent pedaling can really interfere with a musical message; it's like mumbling when you speak. It happens when you sort of "ride" the pedal and get lazy about moving your foot all the way *up* in between. If this is happening to you, I recommend that—at least for a while—you take your foot completely off the pedal and put it to the side until you are confident, through listening, that you are keeping the sonorities distinct and separate, as far as pedaling is concerned.

If you are a still unsure about the proper use of the pedal, a good experiment is to stand up at a grand piano and watch the dampers move as you move the pedal. With an upright (or spinet, console, or studio), open the top lid or in some way expose the hammers and strings so that you can watch the action as you work the pedal. See just how far you need to depress the pedal to initially move the dampers off the strings and what gradations of contact there are with the strings between the dampers all the way up and all the way down. Then go back to allowing the right foot to rest lightly on the pedal, without actually pushing on it at all, as is the normal at-rest position.

Even if you are quite comfortable with pedaling, this is a great exercise. I am a strong believer in knowing *exactly* what is going on mechanically as you play because it helps you to better understand *how* you are making the music you are hearing. The more intimate your connection with the instrument, the finer control you have over it and, accordingly, the more able you are to have it honor your every musical bidding.

The Road Less Traveled

The sustain pedal is a tool that can lend color, reverb-like effects, and interest to your playing. Again, I want you to think outside the normal constraints. Having acquired the skill and practiced the "proper" use of the sustain pedal, it is time to experiment with other uses for it. Often, when I play, I try to do something a little bit different with the sound. I am constantly experimenting with the sustain pedal, trying to sculpt the sound just a little bit differently from the way I did it the last time, to see if I can discover something new. I do in fact often "ride" this pedal *(like I just said you are not supposed to do when you are learning!)* because I use it much of the time for **color**.

One variation you can try with the sustain pedal is the half-pedal, in which you let the dampers just "kiss" the strings. Used in the right way, playing softly, you can create a "faraway" sound. Of course, there are numerous gradations: maybe the dampers barely touch the strings; maybe you let a note ring for a time at half-pedal, and then you release it all the way and cut the sound off. You can let the pedal up abruptly to create a percussive sound.

Perhaps you want to play accented staccato notes *while the sustain pedal is depressed*, or as a variation of this, you could hit a very loud staccato note then press the pedal down immediately *after* you have released the note, catching the *sustain* but not the *attack* of the note.

Another example—when you want to create an impressionistic effect, you can use "sloppy" pedaling. You achieve this by allowing several disparate harmonies to commingle, to waft up into the air and then, while those harmonies are lingering, drop some choice individual notes into the mix, like water droplets into a quiet pool. An easy way to experiment with this particular technique is to play a whole-tone scale (a scale consisting entirely of whole steps) while holding the pedal down *(dampers up!)* the entire time. Play individual notes and clusters (as long as they are part of that scale) and notice as you do this that the sonorities are just happy to merge into each other and coalesce into a lovely, gentle wash of sound. Many of the compositions of Debussy and Ravel are excellent places to examine this type of pedal technique. Listen to Debussy's *Reflets dans l'eau* as an example.

I have also used "sloppy" pedaling in my renditions of some Christmas carols where I wanted to imitate church bell chimes. I wanted to have the different bell tones ring out on top of each other, the way they do live. They needed to sound either as though they were echoing far away or ringing out joyously on top of themselves. Again, the method you use (pedal technique in this case) is subordinate to the effect you want to create. You do whatever is necessary to achieve the emotional experience you are trying to create for the listener. That is what all technique is about. So, it is valuable to know all the different ways you can use the equipment that you already have to create the musical environment you desire at the piano. Another good example to listen to is my arrangement of "Pure Imagination," where in the opening bars I create a wash of sound by holding the pedal down over several bars, and then I drop the melody notes into that backdrop.

Another technique is the "flutter pedal." *(I dislike calling these skills "techniques" because that puts them into the realm of "tricks." They are tools that have to be mastered, certainly, but they have issued from a musical need to create a particular effect and, as such, are part of a musical thrust, not an isolated skill.)* The flutter pedal is what it sounds like. And its use is not confined to a particular musical idiom. Like every other technique, there are a number of ways it can be used. A great way to employ this pedal effect is when, having played a very loud or thick chord or harmony (particularly in the very low register) and you want the notes to last, you can't release the pedal all the way, but you can *thin out the texture* by delicately half-pedaling in a fluttering sort of way, letting the dampers just barely touch the strings until you get a rather sudden *diminuendo* effect in a held sonority—or an actual flutter of the sustained note(s).

Like anything else, this technique is just a tool to be used when appropriate at your discretion—and judiciously so. It shouldn't become a habit, but you should at least acquaint yourself with it. These are all examples of experimenting with novel ways to use common tools. The more equipment at your disposal, the more music you can make.

Side note: The lower you play on the instrument, the less pedal you need to sustain a note. That is primarily due, of course, to the comparative long length of the strings at the lower end. As the strings become shorter, the dampers become lighter, the acoustics change accordingly, and the notes sustain for different lengths of time. One of the most divine qualities of a fine concert grand is the exceedingly long-lasting tone of a note in the middle or upper register when played quietly. However, the acoustical science holds true; the shorter the string, the shorter the sustain. You will notice that as the strings get increasingly shorter toward the top of the instrument, at some point there aren't even any dampers to stop the sound at all since it dies away rather quickly after a note is struck. After a time, the sustain pedal will have become your constant, invisible companion.

"But Soft! What Light through Yonder Window Breaks?"

The "soft" pedal is another wonderful addition to your musical toolbox. The "soft" pedal is actually called the UC (*una corda*) pedal, meaning "one string." It is so called because, on a grand piano, the pedal moves the hammers, and therefore obviously the piano keys, a little bit to the right so that the hammers strike only two of the three strings for each note, thus making the sound quieter without changing its timbre. On an upright-style piano, the hammers are simply moved closer to the strings, so that they cannot generate as much speed hitting the string with the same force; thus, the sound is quieter.

The soft pedal is a joy to use. Once again, let's expand our thinking, this time about what a soft pedal can do, and dispense with some of the constraints that we have come to believe as the only way to do something. The first thing to look at in your effort to use the soft pedal for color and character is to get familiar with what the pedal is actually doing. Take a really close look at the felt heads of the hammers where they contact the strings (this is much more easily seen on a grand piano). You will notice right away that there are "mountains" and "valleys" in them from where the hammer hits the strings in the same exact place over time. Ahh! This at once tells us that we can play with the gradations of moving the hammers with the soft pedal and *control what part of the hammer* hits the string. When we move the soft pedal down all the way (the normal practice, as we have said), the hammer hits just two of the three strings in the "valleys" of the hammer; but if we move the hammer just a touch—about halfway—we make the hammer contact the string on the "mountain" part of the hammer, which is the softer part between the grooves that doesn't get used nearly as much. This is one of the most elegant uses I can think of for the soft pedal. It automatically gives us a *slight* change in timbre, a gentler contact with the string, and is, therefore, another nicety that we can apply to our performance when appropriate. The idea is to try to include as many variations as possible. Practice this by standing as you press the pedal and watching the hammers move on a grand piano. (Sadly, you don't have this option on an upright.) What you are trying to do here is use the soft pedal, not only to play more quietly but to add a new element to the unique personality of your playing.

Here is another oddball use of the soft pedal: sometimes I use this pedal when I am playing *fortissimo*. Why not? I want to change the timbre and have more shades of color at my fingertips. Depending on the instrument and the piece one is playing, this means that the *fortissimo* just acquires a slightly different color with no appreciable loss of volume. Play with it. Don't get caught up in too many rules in your playing. Widen your view and keep expanding your musical mind and your musical tastes.

What Was That Third Pedal Called?

"I Feel Like a Third Wheel . . ."

Oh yeah! The sostenuto pedal. We pianists use this pedal so rarely that a lot of us avoid using it when it could be of great (musical) assistance. Don't think of it as so mysterious that it is rarely used; rather, get so familiar with its use that it becomes just another tool in your music-making repertoire.

If you do not already know, the sostenuto pedal (*sos.*) is used to sustain only those notes that are being held down *while that pedal is depressed*. More precisely, you play the notes you want held, then immediately press the sostenuto pedal, which catches those exact notes *but only those notes*. For example, you may play an octave in the low register that you want to last, but you need two hands to play the next passage. Well, you hold the low note using the sostenuto pedal, and your left hand is now free to tag along with the right and make some music above the lovely lasting low note. Great! The main thing I have to say about this pesky middle pedal is *use it*. Most of us use it rarely, if at all. We just haven't got used to it the way we have with the other two pedals. It is used almost exclusively with the left foot, but don't make that a hard-and-fast rule either.

So, make a habit—for a few weeks, at least—of really practicing the use of that pedal until it is no longer a mysterious, arcane addition to the instrument. Since we are talking about thinking outside the "music box," let's again consider how we can make this pedal another hue in our palette of musical colors.

In addition to the above example, one can—and people often do—use the sustain pedal along with the sostenuto. Experiment with the whole-tone scale exercise I mentioned earlier or try holding an entire chord and then playing lots of staccato passages above it.

As always, with these additions to your musical vocabulary, you will find that you have more freedom to

play it like you mean it.

Chapter 16

SILENCE IS GOLDEN

Say *Nothing* Really *Loud*!

Sometimes you make a point by not saying anything.

Make them wait.

Make

them

wait.

Yes, but what happens during that waiting period?
Glad you asked.

Umm …
Nothing?

Well then, don't do it. You don't just throw silence in there for no reason. Yes, silence is golden, but you have to make it *dynamic* silence. It has to "MOVE"; it has to have a reason to be. How do you accomplish that? How does silence *move*? If you do it right, at the right time, you will be building tension; your listeners will be yearning for the resolution, so that when it finally arrives, it carries with it a satisfying sensation of completion. But why *does* it move us?

Anticipation: Wait for It ...

When you are playing, you know—or expect—what is coming next, and you also know that it will be an answer to a musical question you just posed or an idea you left unfinished. You want it to "come home," as it were.

Side note: You can only do this for so long before the audience says, "Enough already." Like everything else in presenting a work of art, it's a judgment call. A long pause can be very dramatic if people are waiting for the climax, anxiously anticipating the thrilling apex of the melodic line. Then it is much like the end of a sentence or the comforting, satisfying, quiet resolution of a cadence that allows our (metaphorically) held breath to finally expire with a sigh of relief. Our attention is riveted during those silences. But too long a silence can forfeit the listener's attention if it feels like it has no purpose.

So ...
How *long* should a *dramatic* pause be?
How *dramatic* can a *long* pause be?

There are, of course, no answers to those questions. Like any other musical expression, it all depends upon the context, the message, the interpreter, the tempo, and a host of other things. I just want to bring to your attention that *silence* is a genuine participant in communication, not just a "device." Silence has always been used by great orators, such as Churchill.

The kind of long pause I'm talking about tends to happen in **a concert setting**, when everyone in the audience is listening intently. I would rarely use long silences in a casual setting, for example, at a party, or dinner club, or on a recording when you don't know the environment in which it will be heard. You need to know where you are and to whom you are playing.

Here is an example of a dramatic pause within the flow of a communication.

The student tears open her letter from Juilliard. Mom and Dad are waiting, breathless. She reads silently, all the way to the end, her eyes darting from left to right, not betraying any clue to the content. The parents continue to wait, their fingers now entwined, their eyes glued to her every movement, hoping for a clue. She keeps reading. The suspense is unbearable! They want to grab the letter and FIND OUT WHAT IT SAYS! Excruciatingly slowly, she looks up from the letter to her parents and, without a word, hands the letter over and walks silently away as a tear rolls down her cheek. More tense silence as they speed-read the letter.

At last, they come to the long-awaited news: ***She has been accepted to Juilliard!*** Oh, the relief following that dreadful silence! It's almost palpable *(both the silence and the relief).*

Now, visualize *this* scenario: she opens the letter, reads quickly, and about halfway through, says: "Good news! I've been accepted to Juilliard! What's for dinner?"

'Nuff said?

Dynamic, living, breathing silence. Do it.

Chapter 17

PRACTICE

Then Can I Go to the Movies?

The Basics

This is one of the most important sections in this book. I stress here again that my intention is not to countermand anything that your teacher has taught you about how to practice. My hope is that you are getting excellent instruction on all of this from your teacher or your college professor, someone who is guiding you to become a better musician. So, my suggestions here are not so much about how to actually practice the piano. What I want to do is to help you look at all those ancillary things about practice that I have learned from 50 years of doing both right and wrong things.

Here is an overview of how I approach learning a new piece of music.

Practice Makes...um...Better...

As you begin your practice of any new piece, get the idea that the purpose of the first run-through is simply to acquaint you with the piece in its entirety. As you go through, read the best that you can, make all sorts of mis-readings, mistakes, and fingering faux pas; just keep going and get a good "feel" for what it is going to be like when you can finally play it properly. Won't *that* be fun!

Having done this a few times, start to notice the scheme or layout. Are there passages that repeat exactly? (Yay! You don't have to learn *that* part all over again!) Are there some places that already fall under the hand so naturally that you know you are not going to have a problem with them at speed? Are there particular places at which you expect to encounter technical difficulties? On and on, noticing how this wonderful puzzle is put together.

As you work on learning the overall piece, practice and perfect, to the best of your ability, the greater part of the music that is *not* challenging, so that you can get through almost all of it except for those few problem places. This will give you confidence and a feeling of achievement, which you will have earned. In addition, you will feel that you know most of the piece with just a few bad spots, instead of just thinking "This whole piece is really difficult!" By the way, as you are moving through this process, you will discover perks along the way. You are actually beginning the process of *memorizing* the piece without thinking about it.

Also, as far as getting a passage up to speed, remember that *fast* playing is achieved by *slow* playing. It's fun to play fast. It's like running fast when you are a kid. It's just fun, even if you stumble. But when you really want to play a fast passage accurately, you need to play it slowly enough at first to gain **certainty**. Gaining certainty at a slow tempo is how you gain speed.

*Side note: Notes played **accurately** sound faster than sloppy notes played at a faster tempo. Never sacrifice sacred accuracy at the altar of the graven image of speed.*

An Observation: The Brick Wall

I have noticed that during the learning process in a given practice session, I will make a great deal of progress at first. Then after some unspecified time, the piece starts to get worse. I start making mistakes that I didn't make earlier in the process. When that happens to you, be neither concerned nor puzzled.

It just happens—at least to me. It is a manifestation of staying on one idea or section too long. I don't know, and I don't care why—it happens. It just happens. So don't agonize about it. Don't try to figure it out. Maybe you have had enough of learning that passage for now, and your brain needs time to process. Let it do its work. While that part of the brain-soup is simmering in the background, you can get a lot else done with other parts of the score. The remedy is to just *leave it alone*. Don't stress over it. Go on to something else; there is always plenty to study. An hour, a day, a week later, it will have worked itself out, and you can continue the learning process on that phrase or portion of the music.

The mind is a remarkable mechanism, capable of multitasking subconsciously, while you consciously give it other tasks. It is a wonderful machine. Don't diminish its abilities by trying to make it do something that it can already do without your bidding.

Gosh! I've Missed You Sooooo Much! (And So Often!)

Missing the same notes over and over again? Don't you just hate that? You've been working on this piece for several months now, and yet you keep messing up at the very same place! Well, at some time you have to just cry uncle *and never play that piece again ever in your whole life or in the future history of the universe, in perpetuity!*

OR—and this is a better idea—figure out once and for all what is happening. This is the time to put on your deerstalker hat and do some serious detective work. Where *exactly* are you tripping over a note or two? In order to fix it *so that it never happens again,* you need to know what *it* is. That means using an aural/visual magnifying glass.

Hurry Up and Slow Down!

Usually (*usually!*), there are one or two bars of the music that are accounting for most of the problems, sometimes even just a couple of notes. The thought is "I can't play this phrase," when the reality is "I don't even know precisely where I am screwing up."

Try playing the whole passage deathly slow. What do I mean by "deathly slow"? I mean "deathly slow." So slow that you can't hear any phrase or melody or harmony.

Like   reading

              this   as   just   a

jumble of

              disconnected words.

(think e. e. cummings.)

Why do this? Because by playing this slowly, you are taking away the automatic response that has caused you to glaze over the hard part in the first place. You are defeating muscle memory. It's like singing "My country, *'tisofthee....*" You learn the sound as a child and mimic it, but what's a " 'tisofthee" anyway? When one day (*or never*) you find out that those are three separate words, why, then you have gained understanding and knowledge of the meaning of the song. With that song, it doesn't really matter. But with the classical piece you are playing, you must *know* what you are singing or playing about. When you defeat *automaticity,* you are forced to actually *learn* the passage.

You need to isolate which exact note, notes, or span of notes are giving you the problem. Often you will find that it is not the notes you originally thought. Sometimes, you may discover that the *right*-hand part is the real problem, when all along you were messing up in the *left* hand. In a wide leap, you are probably concentrating on hitting the destination, but you may find out that it was the jumping off point that you are not sure of. Or it may be that the passage *leading up* to the apparent problem is the real ogre.

How do I know this? Don't ask. The point is this sort of exercise makes your brain work differently. That strategy (reflex action of the fingers) can get you by a lot of the time, but when you stumble, you are adrift without a paddle, if you get my drift. That can't happen if you actually *know* each note.

Now let's consider another aspect of your overall practice routine.

What do you intend to do with your music in the long term? *Um ... I dunno ...*

Before you try to come up with a regimen for practicing, you need to understand *why* you want to play piano in the first place. Of course, because you enjoy it, but in order to figure out a really beneficial ongoing practice routine, you need to be more specific. So, ask yourself what your long-term goals are and find your own fulfilling answers. Be honest with yourself. Spend some time on this little exercise because it will be a guiding principle in all your future practice. *It is the reason you practice the way that you do. So, what's it for?*

Is it for the pure joy of playing?

Is it to teach others how to create on this wonderful instrument?

Is it to perform on the concert stage?

For example, are you preparing your senior recital for the spring semester? Well then, spend all of your time perfecting that repertoire.

On the other hand, if you are just playing piano as a hobby for your own enjoyment, maybe to perform for a few friends, you don't need a schedule at all; just play when you feel like it and be gentle with yourself.

On the other, *other* hand, maybe you want to get a job as a cocktail pianist. Well, then you need to learn as many old standards as possible in as short a time as possible, well enough to play through them by memory or by ear. No sheet music. No real arrangements, per se. No need to perfect each one. You will be getting requests, and you need to know the age range of your audience and what songs they are likely to ask for. In cocktail piano, the American songbook is a staple in everyone's musical diet, then big songs from musicals, movies, and current top 40 songs.

If you want to be a professional accompanist, you'd better learn to be an excellent sight reader of both classical and pop, full sheet music and fake charts. You must be able to transpose at sight and learn the fine points of accompanying, which is a skill that is different from that of playing solo. We discuss the art of accompaniment in Part Two of this book.

If you want to accompany ballet classes, as I did, you will need to be able to improvise in a classical style, and acquire an in-depth knowledge of the strict tempo, phrase length, and stylistic requirements of the traditional ballet barre exercises, plus their (French) names.

If your goal is to be an entertainer, you'll need to develop a versatile technique and evolve a personalized style. You'll need to become great at playing by ear and experimenting with many genres of music.

If you want to have your own show on the concert stage, you will need to learn to write scripts, create a great program, understand that you will need to potentially entertain an audience for two hours all by yourself, and hold the audience's interest throughout the entire evening.

In all these cases, it's never too soon to start honing these skills, in *addition* to what your teacher gives you to study.

You get the idea: "form follows function." This is especially true with practicing the piano. We all begin the same way. When you start learning piano, the purpose of your introductory lessons is to acquaint you with the instrument, find your way around its mechanical properties, get to know the "feel" of pushing the keys, learn to read, and get some basic skills into your brain and fingers. But after the first few years, you need to have a good long look at what it is you ultimately hope to *do* with your music, so that, *in addition to doing what your teacher is having you do,* you can start spending some of your practice time directed toward a specific discipline. A conversation around the above questions will help you decide how to best use your practice time.

- There are many ways to practice, and I will make a few suggestions, but in order to practice "properly" (to efficiently use your time) *you need to know what you are trying to achieve.* I can't stress this enough. So reread the above short descriptions and decide in which **general** direction you want to go, recognizing, of course, that this can change over time. Then, when you go to the practice room, you will have a goal in mind.

Advil? We Don't Need No Stinkin' Advil!

Your fingers, wrists, arms, shoulders, and back should *never* get exhausted or injured from practicing the piano. Does that sound ridiculous? Strange? Not true?

I am not talking about that great muscular glow that you feel after a hard workout at the gym or the feeling of strength and exhilaration that follows a several-hour-long practice session. Those are good feelings that let you know you have been developing muscle and getting stronger. I am talking about actual aches and pains—hurting yourself.

For a start, let me reiterate that your teacher will have told you his or her approach to the best posture, hand and arm position, and so on. By all means, follow that. They know what they are doing. The purpose of this advice is to get you to a *mental* place that allows you to play for hours without physical strain. If you begin to feel strain or tiredness, have a look at what you may be doing *mentally* that is causing the distress. Often it is the stress of approaching a particularly demanding passage, the anxiety of meeting a deadline, or frustration because a certain technical challenge seems to persist no matter what you do. Any number of mental attitudes can make your muscles tense up, often just before you get to the challenging place in the music—the measures or run that you are already predisposed to mess up. That anxiety can translate into physical discomfort and even pain or possible injury. When you are practicing out of *fear* instead of *understanding*, you are inhibiting your progress.

That said, it *is* a fact that you are using muscles and training them in new directions. However, *what you are really training is your* **mind**. And minds don't get muscle fatigue.

There are two aspects of muscular motion that I would like you to investigate. The first is a purely physical one. In playing any note, and series of notes, please remember—and practice—that immediately after you have pushed the key down all the way, you have only to hold it down with the lightest touch to keep it from coming back up. You do not have to continue to press it. Once the hammer has hit the string, there is nothing you can do to affect the sound. So why waste energy? It is the continual pressure on a key, once it has done its job of creating a sound, that leads to tiredness, fatigue, and muscle strain. It does not take a lot of *strength* to play the piano; it takes a lot of intelligently directed effort. It is the pushing of the key and then the *instant relaxing* that allows you to play for hours on end. As we spoke about in the chapter on dynamics, it takes almost no pressure at all to keep a key on the piano depressed once you have made a sound. In this way, you are conserving enormous amounts of energy, and you will be able to play longer and more efficiently without your fingers, wrists, or arms getting tired. You can play for hours and not hurt yourself. If you are a serious student of piano, you will *have* to play for hours on end, so you do not want to do something that can lead toward injury.

The other way to conserve energy and muscular strength is to recognize that you are playing piano with your *mind*, not just with your physical strength. If you care to explore this idea in depth, I highly recommend reading the book *New Pathways to Piano Technique* by Luigi Bonpensiere, published in 1953.

Here is the basic premise. You familiarize yourself intimately with the layout of the keyboard. You learn it in detail intellectually. In other words, you have learned the basics of piano playing. We start from there. The *traditional* procedure is to then exhaustively train your muscles to do as they are told by doing the same motions over and over to produce the results that you want.

Here is the great divide. In the approach in the above-mentioned book, in the principle proposed, which the author calls "ideo-kinetics" (physical motion initiated by mental ideation), he suggests that the body, which accomplishes incredibly complex actions on a routine basis through the autonomic nervous system—things such as breathing, walking, the blood flow throughout our bodies—without our even being aware of it, already knows the most efficient way of accomplishing a fairly straightforward physical motion, such as playing the piano. Thus, in this way of thinking, why not just tell the body what you wish to accomplish? Hear the notes, understand them and, essentially, say to the body: "This is what I want to hear. Now produce that sound at the piano, thank you very much."

Given that you have a thorough knowledge of the keyboard and an understanding of what it is you are trying to accomplish musically, *you now leave it to the body to figure out the most efficient way to do it.* That is the difference. You may find that your inner body intelligence guides you into a new hand position or a fingering you never thought of. Hence the title, *New Pathways to Piano Technique*. It is worth a look.

I know on first reading that this may sound like theoretical philosophy. But there is actually a practical application of that premise. You might be surprised at the inherent wisdom that the body already possesses. Your attention should be on the substance of the piece you are playing, not the mechanics. It is quite wonderful. There are things we can do, ways that we can touch the keys to consciously aid the body's natural intelligence, certainly. But beyond that—and, I believe, far more to the point—there is a necessary paradigm shift that is senior to all of that.

I only discovered ideo-kinetics when I was in my 40s; so, in my own playing, I use a combination of techniques from the more traditional way I was trained in my formative years (hours and hours of dedicated practice to achieve the most efficient use of muscular strength) and the ideo-kinetic approach of creating a musical "fiat" and asking the body to do my bidding.

Let every practice session be one of joy. I really mean that. You are learning, even if it's at a snail's pace, how the composer created this beautifully complex piece of architecture for you to explore, imbibe, and eventually command. This is so that one day you will be able to explain, through sound alone, what was on the composer's mind and heart as he wrote down these notes, sequences, and sublime melodies that resonate with listeners long after his death. You are continuing a legacy, whether it be that of a Beethoven, a Rodgers and Hammerstein, or a Gershwin. You are part of a stream of art and life, and all the work you have done to arrive at this hallowed place is coalescing and culminating into your opportunity to propel that legacy into the future. Relieved of the intricacies of muscular coordination, now relinquished to the body's innate intelligence, you are left to create music freely and to more easily

play it like you mean it.

Chapter 18

MENTAL PRACTICE

Mental Practice Doesn't Mean You're "Mental"

If you are often awake at night, like I am, well, you need something to do while you are staring at the back of your eyelids thinking of all the stupid things you've done in your life. When that ceases to be fun, I suggest you mentally practice the pieces you are working on while you lie there wishing you could go back to sleep. Start "playing" in your mind a piece that is difficult for you and pay attention to every note. (This is also a good way to memorize a piece.)

Some things to be aware of while you are doing this exercise:

As you "play" through in your mind, notice where you are not sure of *exactly* what comes next; which precise note, or chord, or phrase makes you stumble mentally? You see, your actual, *physical* practice at the keyboard—if you are practicing properly—is about 80 percent mental anyway. Your fingers have to learn how to wiggle, certainly, but most of your technique is coming from a genuine understanding of the notes and structure of the chords and sequences of notes that you are playing. So, as you practice in your mind, you will find either blank spaces where you truly don't know where to go next or places that you usually sort of skim over at the piano and afterward don't really know exactly what has happened. This mental practice can help you focus in, laser-like, to the actual problem areas.

It is also important to be very careful when you are rehearsing in your mind that you do not practice bad habits. By this I mean that as you encounter a part of the piece that gives you trouble, don't *expect* in your mind to play it incorrectly or feel your fingers making the same mistakes you make at the piano. ***Don't practice your mistakes.*** Don't stumble in your mind when you come to a difficult passage and then come back to speed just after it just like you did at the piano earlier that day. Don't gloss over or *pretend not to see (hear)* a passage that you "sort of" know. Instead, use this mental play to find out *exactly* what you need to do next time you are seated at the instrument.

Sometimes when I do this, my fingers want to move—at least mentally—and, sure enough, they trip where they trip at the piano when I'm running through it in my mind. What I do then is **sit on my hands** (in my mind—I'm serious about this) and play a mental recording of the passage the way I would like to hear it if someone else were playing it. Because if I am sitting on my hands, so to speak, the physical stuttering can't interfere. What we are doing here is getting intimately familiar with the piece. Because when you play it **only** mentally, you can't rely on muscle memory (which is a stimulus-response memory), and you don't have the notes in front of you. You have to *know* it. And this is a great way to find out what you *don't know.*

On the other hand, if you really need to go to sleep immediately, day or night, just read the above paragraph a couple of times and—guaranteed—you will slip into dreamland! I nearly dozed off while writing it!

Hope this helps!

Chapter 19

THE DOLDRUMS

I'll Sure Be Glad When I've Had Enough of This!

There you are, sitting at the piano, wishing the clock would move faster, working on a recital piece that is due all too soon. Your mind is wandering; your legs are cramping; you are bored to tears—you want to be any other place at all. The clock is ticking away, and the days are getting closer together as you approach your deadline. *Sheesh! It's like a final exam!* It *is* a final exam! And even though you have six more weeks, you are starting to worry. You *know* you have to learn this new piece of music. You know you should want to practice. You know you are capable of playing it, *but you just don't feel like practicing*. You go to the piano, but you don't want to be there. But you know you need to meet the deadline, or you will be in deep trouble!

You have hit the **doldrums.** So, what do you do?
What *DO* you do?

There are several ways to handle this.
Try to get out of it.

Run away!

Move to another state!

Give up playing piano altogether!

Tell your teacher:

"My pet goat ate all my sheet music!"

"I really didn't want to be a pianist in the first place."

"I have to rearrange my sock drawer that night."

"I am an undercover agent for the DEA, and I have to fly to Venezuela that evening to raid a drug cartel. Playing piano was just a cover."

Oh, so you've tried all those already? Sorry.

Failing all of those incredibly creative fixes, you know you HAVE to play the piece for the recital, concert, event, whatever—you absolutely *have* to.

YOU CAN'T GET OUT OF IT.

Well, that is the time for what I call …

TA-DA!

"Digging a Ditch"
(Too bad!)

You have to do it. You have to get "Nike" about it: *just do it.* I know, I know—that's not the answer you were hoping for. Me neither. Here's what I suggest you do. You know by now that I like metaphors.

Let's say you are in your backyard, and you have to dig a ditch to install a sprinkler system. The day is hot; the ground is like cement, and your shovel is dull. You wipe your brow, take the shovel in hand, push down with all your might, and make a slight dent in the ground. You keep doing this until you have a small furrow, about a 100th of the way down to where you need to dig. While you are thus engaged in this joyless, thankless chore, you think of sunny beaches, cool mountain lakes, what's-her-name in high school, or wherever your "happy place" is, and you just keep digging or at least pushing the dirt around. And you know what? At the end of the hour or two hours or three, you have the beginnings of a ditch. I promise, you will look back proudly and say, very sincerely, "Well, that sure sucked!"

Here's the reason: when thinking about practicing, you are looking at the entire piece (a 100-foot ditch) instead of just reading the first note on the page (the first little "dimple" in the hardened ground). When the score is technically demanding, it can seem overwhelming.

But how do you dig a *musical* ditch? You need to just start playing the notes of the new piece mindlessly and, most of all, SLOWLY *reading the notes on the paper*.

Here's what is happening: your mind may be elsewhere—you might be thinking of 10 other things—*but a part of your attention is needed so that you can read the notes.* You are not interested in what it sounds like. Just put in the hours and give as much attention as possible to what you are doing while mentally sitting in the sun. I'm serious about this. And tomorrow is another day of ditchdigging. And I promise you that tomorrow will be better than today. You've made a dent. You've learned one or two notes of this difficult or boring piece of music. Seriously. Try it.

This is the best time to remember that *you are making progress even if you can't see any progress.* Synapses are synapsing (or whatever synapses do for fun) while you are off in Never-Never Land, just pushing the keys around. Remember, you are feeding data into your seemingly idle brain. Something is happening. You will be very surprised—I promise you—at what you will have learned from doing this mindless exercise. I use classical music for this example simply because the technical demands are usually more challenging. But, of course, it works for any type of music.

You are digging a musical ditch. In a few days or weeks, you will have at least a hole in the ground. A trench, a crease, a crinkle. A furrow—like the one on your brow as you read this.

"Yup! See that dent? I did that. Only took me three days."

Did you enjoy digging it? I dunno … probably not, but if you are like me, you have the satisfaction of knowing that you now know a new piece of music—or at least a *piece* of a piece of music. And you can give yourself a well-deserved pat on the back for having gone through an exercise of self-discipline that makes you feel proud of yourself (even if you haven't mastered the music yet). It's a good feeling. *"I did it anyway!"*

Usually when I do this, there is a point at which the piece or song captures my attention, and then I *want* to practice it. **And by then, I am out of the doldrums.**

Then, lo and behold! One day, a few days or weeks later, you will be amazed at how much you have learned. All you are doing in this exercise is putting some notes into your fingers, your brain, and, interestingly, into your memory. You aren't performing it; you are not being musical about it yet. You are just learning the notes.

It is also an exercise in **multitasking** *(the day at the beach plus those darned notes)*. After that we head back into our "normal" practice routine. Now you can learn it enjoyably for real. Tweak it; make it musical—all those things you do to prepare a piece of music for performance. I am in no way recommending that you approach everyday practice this way. As I said in Chapter 17, practice time spent at the piano should be a joy!

This method, device, strategy is but a stopgap measure for when you cannot muster the "umph" to practice but you *have* to. I hope you never find yourself there, but you probably will from time to time … so if you do, well, it ain't that bad!

So, there you have it. One mindless step at a time to dig your way out of the doldrums.

P.S. During the doldrums, don't even *try* to

play it like you mean it.

Good luck.

Chapter 20

HOW TO GET INSPIRED

Inspiration and Perspiration

Let's talk about inspiration—or a lack thereof. Not feeling inspired is a familiar problem to most people at some time or other in their creative endeavors, careers, hobbies, or in life in general. Here is a pertinent question that someone asked me a few years ago.

"So, I've been in a piano slump lately, and I wonder what a professional like yourself does to get inspired again? I feel like it's really difficult to play romantic music when I'm just not 'feeling' it and wonder what kind of muses or sources of inspiration pros have to reignite their passions?"

Ho–hum …

First of all, don't worry about the slump parts. There are hundreds of reasons as to why that happens, and unless a slump just drags on and on, just think "this, too, shall pass." Slumps are part of life. Sometimes you may not want to work on your painting for a few days or weeks, go to the gym, or do your laundry. When that happens, you don't necessarily assume something is wrong (nothing *is* wrong); it's just a passing thing of no real significance.

The takeaway here is that you must try not to make it into a big deal. It happens, and there are ways to deal with it. Don't exacerbate the condition by chiding yourself or wondering what's wrong with you. Newsflash— nothing is "wrong" with you. A slump happens to *everybody* at some time. There is absolutely nothing amiss about not wanting to play the piano for a while. You are not unlearning the piano by not playing for a few days or even weeks. Just remind yourself that it's not a big deal.

That said, we still want to do something about it. So, here are some suggestions for getting reinspired.

1. Go through your music library and revisit some of the music that you have loved over the years, listening to songs or classical pieces or playing them yourself, *not for the purpose of getting inspired* but just for the pure enjoyment of listening. Get on with your work; enjoy your life and listen to the music that makes your heart soar. Find new music from friends. Revisit your own recording collection. Just listen to a lot of music.

2. Look at your favorite artwork or read poetry if that's your thing. Remember that wonderful "How do I love thee ..." poem you heard in school all those years ago recited by a favorite teacher who really *understood* Elizabeth Barrett Browning? Read it again with a new perspective from being that much older and wiser.

3. Imagine what you would be like if you could be whatever you wanted to be. Think about how you would make the world a prettier place; think in poetic terms. Rhapsodize! Maybe watch a movie that inspires you to be more than you are. Go away from the piano and just surround your intellectual-emotional self with other art forms: literature, sculpture, architecture, painting, film, or dance. (*Riverdance* is a great suggestion.) Whatever makes your eyes widen and your heart beat faster. Maybe read stories of people who overcame incredible odds to summit Mount Everest or to design a better mousetrap. Search for people doing things that are way out of the ordinary.

Guaranteed, at some point, something will trigger you, and you will say, "I must learn that piece," or "I have to get to a piano and just try out this one simple motif or technique." You may wonder about the composer—How'd he *do* that?—and then you might feel that you *must* get to the piano to try to work out the puzzle. Perhaps you will get an idea for an arrangement, or ... or—

OR NOT.

That is not the point. *The point is to reopen what has become a temporarily closed mind,* to widen your view. A slump happens because we are focused too narrowly on exactly what we are doing, to the point of becoming introverted and tunnel visioned. What we are trying to do in this little exercise is reawaken a dormant area of our minds, broaden our view, realize there is a whole world out there that has nothing to do with our troubled little universe, and attain a more holistic view of our lives in general—at least for a while.

4. Learn that *you* are the master of your mind's direction and that of your spirit and are thereby imbibing some tiny particle of what the vast universe of creativity has to offer simply by being around it or being immersed in it, as you are in life, whether you consciously seek it out or not. "I am the master of my fate; I am the captain of my soul." (Thank you, Mr. Henley.)

All that circumlocution aside, this suggestion is simply:

Immerse yourself in art and music all over again.

Think back to a time when you were infatuated with another person, and you noticed every little detail about her or him that enchanted you: the way she tossed her hair away from her eyes, the way he smiled at you, the timbre of her voice, the way his eyes scrunched up when he laughed, the funny little twinkle in her eye when she told a joke, or his awkwardness at meeting a new person.

The piano is no different. It is your close, intimate friend. If you sometimes neglect each other, as can happen with a close friend, it doesn't mean your friendship has suffered irreparably. It's just another chapter in your journey. Learning to be away from your loved one for a time is part of any maturing relationship. You shouldn't feel guilty about leaving the piano alone; you shouldn't look the other way, embarrassedly, as you pass it by. You must realize nothing has changed, and you are still buddies. You don't have to do anything together right now; just remind yourself that this part of your life is always there for you. Remember, the piano is a lifelong friend! How many friends do you have like that? Do this little mental-emotional exercise until you have fallen in love with the piano again.

If you have never done this before, how do you actually accomplish this? Well, here's how I do it.

I walk over to the piano with no agenda except to marvel at the wonder of the instrument. I don't necessarily play anything, just touch it, walk around it, and admire it as a piece of **artwork** (*which it very much is! It is an iconic shape! Nothing else in this world is shaped like a grand piano!*) that has nothing to do with me. Then I *forgive myself* for not wanting to be near it that day, go back to what I was doing, and get on with my life. I find a different project to work on, another chore that needs doing. Maybe I take out the garbage or fix that leaky faucet. When I can finally allow myself the luxury of *no self-chastisement* on the subject, I can look more analytically at the problem at hand. In other words, I have stopped berating myself for what is a normal response in life, removed the psychological *(or shall we call it "psycho-**illogical**"?)* barrier to the "can't-get-inspired" syndrome, and am left with the actual situation, which is: I have a deadline; I need to handle this chore in an intelligent way *without the added burden of entangling myself in the trappings of emotional nonsense.* Now it is a matter of applying self-discipline dispassionately to the task before me (see the previous chapter, "Digging a Ditch").

So, there you have it. If you find yourself in a dead zone creatively, turn your inner focus to enjoying art for the sake of art, i.e., becoming inspired. When you feel emboldened and revitalized, go back to the piano, sit down and

play it like you mean it.

Chapter 21

MEMORIZING

What Were We Talking About?

In learning a piece of music by heart, I don't place my faith entirely in memorization—I depend mostly on *understanding*. By that, I mean that I do not treat memorization as a separate skill or discipline. It happens automatically as I am learning and understanding the piece I am working on.

That said, let's have a look at the different types of memorization techniques: muscle, rote, visual, aural, emotional, and intellectual. All of these are valid and are normally used in combination; and in my view, they are all paths to true understanding and, therefore, dependable memory.

Muscle Memory: *"Strong! Like Bull!"*

Muscle memory is a special type of memory. There are a thousand great uses for it in life. For example, every time you get in your car, whether you are talking to someone, thinking of a hundred different things, or remembering your shopping list, you nonetheless—and unerringly—stick the key in the ignition without looking at it or thinking about it. It happens every time you start up the car. Think about it: you are putting that very slender key into a very slender keyhole that you cannot even see (in most cars), and you do it perfectly every time. *(I hate to say this, but now that I have mentioned it—once you start thinking about it, you may find that next time you try you will miss the keyhole because you are defeating muscle memory by thinking of where to put the key. Sorry! But I had to make a point.)*

There are numerous uses for muscle memory that are entirely automatic (how you put on your clothes in the morning or how you reach for a light switch in the dark). Mindless tasks are taken care of so that you don't have to waste precious brain power on everyday actions. In its proper place, muscle memory is a wonderful mechanism that works automatically on little, insignificant things with next to no effort on our part to train it.

When it comes to sophisticated actions like playing the piano, that is a different story. It takes years of ongoing training to instill into our neurological pathways whatever it is that complies with our wishes so that, at last, our bodies respond physically to our mental commands with seemingly no intermediary. You ask your hand to play an F-major triad, and it does. You don't have to wiggle your fingers around till you get it right.

However, muscle memory has limitations. It works beautifully for physical technique (arm, hand, fingers, and so on). But some people make the mistake of thinking that they can use muscle memory to *learn* a piece of music. That is a mistake because you cannot train a group of muscles to understand a piece of music. You can't rely on muscle memory alone when you are playing the piano because you're playing real live music in real live clock time. You are creating on the fly. Muscle memory will not allow for minute changes in physical actions. It relies on the premise that you will do the same motion exactly the same way every time. That is simply not realistic. When something unexpected happens, muscle memory will let you down.

Suppose you are playing, and you are relying upon what your body remembers to do, but there's a sudden noise or some other distraction. Or you're performing onstage, and at the edge of your peripheral vision, you see someone get up and walk out of the hall. These sorts of intrusions of outside influences on a rehearsed muscular reaction can throw it off the routine. It is like the fabled door-to-door salesman who has his spiel memorized, but if he gets interrupted, he has to start all over from the beginning. Why? Because it's not *known*—it's not understood. It's memory relying on muscle memory—even if it's brain muscle being trained (figuratively).

However, there are certainly times that muscle memory can come in handy at the piano. If I'm relearning a piece of music that I haven't played for many years, and I don't have the sheet music available, I can start playing the part I remember. When I come to a place where I can't think of what comes next, I purposely take my attention off it. My hands know what to do even though my brain doesn't, as long as I don't interfere. After two or three tries, muscle memory manages to play the missing parts, and I watch my fingers as though I am separate from them and see what notes they just played. Then I can begin to relearn that part the right way.

So, yes, muscle memory certainly has a place in learning and is one ingredient in the memorizing process, but true memorizing is something else entirely.

Rote Memory: *That's All She Rote...*

And that's all you will remember if you use this method.

We all know what rote memory is: our times tables, capitals of states, names of presidents, and so on. These are all bits of information that are valuable and useful but that we don't need or want to think about. Learning these things is a "pure memory" exercise with no obligatory understanding of what we are memorizing. As a training exercise for the "mind at play," it's a delightful activity, and probably sharpens you up, but has no real place in memorizing music, except perhaps as an unconscious mental activity that plays a very small part in overall memorizing.

I think of this sort of memorizing as the brain's version of muscle memory. To my way of thinking, it is a utilitarian skill that can be learned and enhanced by practice, but it really has very little application to the art of piano playing, or any creative art, for that matter.

Visual Memory: Your Face Looks Familiar . . .

I have known at least one person who is able to "see" in his mind, very accurately, the printed page of music, and then he can simply "read" the music in front of him and thus not really need to *memorize* as such. If you are one of the fortunate ones who can do this, then your path to memorizing has been shortened by a great deal. That is a wonderful ability that I do not possess. This advanced type of full visual memory is, in my experience, rare, but I think we all have it to some slight degree. When I encounter a passage that gives me a great deal of trouble, I will look at the page very deliberately and very consciously try to create an image of it that I can refer to later on. For me, it is normally a measure or two, and when I need to, for example, at night as I am going to sleep, I can call up that image and study the exact sequence of notes and thus do some mental memorizing as I drift off to sleep.

Aural Memory: That Song Keeps Playing in My Head! Make It Stop!

Much more common is your aural memory, as, after all, that is what music is all about. We all rely to a greater or lesser degree on aural memory and use it to direct our fingers as we are learning. When you actively focus your attention on how the music sounds in *every detail* (not just in an overall impression of the piece), so that you can approximate a part of it without the notes, then you are on your way to including musical interpretation as you memorize, for you will sing a line in your head along with your concept of how it should sound. We do it automatically. It is a great subconscious tool that we all use to memorize a new piece of music. It is akin to playing by ear. I say "akin" because there are not too many individuals who can hear a complex classical piece of music and play it back note for note. However, you cannot help hearing the notes as you are learning them.

The use of aural memory is a tool that helps you work out what the exact notes are in your mind when you are away from the piano. You almost don't have to think about it; you will just find yourself mentally hearing the piece you are working on. It just happens. The thing to watch out for is "rehearsing" a mistake. Often, when we idly sing a piece of music in our heads, we are doing only a close approximation of it. So, if you find that as you "sing" through it, there are a few places where you are unsure, go back to the sheets, carefully look at the dots, and commit those few exact notes to memory by saying them aloud or repeating to yourself the *exact* notes of that chord until you are confident that you have them understood and "heard" them correctly.

Emotional Memory: *I'll Never Forget What's-Her-Name...*

When I am starting to learn a new piece of music that I am truly excited about, I will often get the sheet out and just bungle my way through it the best I can, just to experience the *emotion* of the thing. The "Oh-my-gosh!" feeling, knowing that "someday I will be able to play this thing and make people feel what I am feeling right now!" At that point it time, I want to play it over and over, and I can't stop right then to get the notes right. I just want to fumble around, get the adrenaline going, be there in the practice room all by myself, without anyone to hear which notes I may have missed, and just barrel ahead in the pure, unbridled joy of creating some semblance of the amazing music that is on the page in front of me.

It's all about how I *feel* when I do that. It's exhilarating! A restorative tonic for the emotional soul. Just what you need every now and then. Get it out of your system! When *I* do this, I do look at the printed page, but I just *guess* at the notes that I can't sight-read, approximate what I don't yet understand, and act like I already know the piece. I don't care how awful it sounds; I am getting into the spirit, the viscera of the piece, the emotional nitty-gritty! I bang out enough to get the blood flowing and imagine myself playing this wonderful creation of Chopin long before I actually can play it. I do this for as long as I like, until I am satiated with the glorious sensation of abandon and emotional liberation from any sort of "rules" of practice. This gives me the *oomph* to go on to the real work of actually *learning* the piece. I then can't *wait* to learn it! When you inject emotion into the practice session, the process of memorization has already begun because you are remembering the notes or phrases that you formed an emotional bond with.

Phew!

Intellectual Memory: *Shouldn't That Be a Hemidemisemiquaver?*

Let's apply this section to the study of a new piece of music, especially a particularly daunting classical one, one that you never thought you could master. Maybe, in your musical education, you had always figured that a particular piece was forever beyond your capabilities, so you never even considered looking at the music. You secretly wished you could play it, but it was forever out of reach; you never even *tried!*

Well, I am here to encourage you to *try!* Think of it as an exercise of will and brain power. We want to revise your mental attitude toward the music from one of fear and intimidation to one of triumph and elation as it is the application of one's *intellect* to a perceived problem that leads to a thorough understanding of what has appeared till now to be a paralyzing conundrum.

Intellectual memorizing—or should I say, *learning*—involves diligent and rational study, the goal of which is to truly wrap one's wits around the musical *mystery* facing one at a given moment. It is quite the opposite of *emotional* learning.

It is the mind diligently working out a puzzle of some sort (in this instance a musical one). So, you begin by looking meticulously at the minutiae, one note, chord, phrase, or measure at a time, until you have wrested from the printed page *why* the notes were written down the way they were and *how* the composer put those notes into a mosaic that culminates in a real-world realization of what he heard in his head (all those centuries ago!). Why, then it becomes a pure joy to learn. "*Oh my! How did he even think of that sequence of notes?*" "*So **that's** how he did it!*" What a feeling of satisfaction and achievement you will experience having bested this wonderful, lovable adversary!

When you look at it that way, it is an adventure, a riddle you are solving; it is invigorating to play this cerebral game. *And a game is what it is at this point!* You are Sherlock Holmes ferreting out the secrets that lie hidden in this wondrous, frustrating jumble of notes. You have deduced, through careful inspection, the answers to what was heretofore but a chaos of confusion, and you have emerged victorious! You will congratulate yourself; you will feel smarter—because you *are* smarter now, by *that much!* Oh! The feeling of well-deserved pride in such an accomplishment is delicious indeed! You have earned an honorary crown of laurels. And although this may only be round one in a long contest, you can take a break, indulge in a little happy dance, and go back into the fray ready for round two, equipped with the gratifying knowledge that you are genuinely stronger now, *not weaker*, after this (possibly exhausting) mental contest because you now know how the game is played. Suddenly, these pages before you are no longer shrouded in a cloak of mystery, rather they appear as an exciting, gift-wrapped surprise just waiting to be discovered by you!

You have completed the most difficult part of the exercise: **you have changed your mind.**

Putting It All Together: True Memorizing—*Now I Remember!*

So, what do I believe is the most dependable way to memorize something? The type of memory that will never fail you is the kind that comes from true *understanding*. If you study a piece of music, be it classical or pop, to a point where you could *recreate* it (approximately), not from memory but, rather, from *knowing* it intimately, why, then you never have to go through the separate exercise of "memorizing."

To elaborate: think back to telling a friend about some event that actually *happened* to you. You don't have to memorize it; you KNOW it. It is part of your history, and what you KNOW, you don't forget.

To summarize, here are some tips on how to actually go about memorizing a piece of (classical) music that is challenging.

First of all, read through the whole piece, or a section of a longer piece, to familiarize yourself with it overall. From being a stranger, it has now become an acquaintance. Just get a feel for it. Take a sort of architectural, holistic approach to studying it. You are using all your visual, aural, and intellectual faculties at this point.

Now we get into more detail. Admire the beauty of a particular harmony, a subtle voice leading, or a particularly agile sequence of notes; describe it to yourself in words. Look in awe at the beauty of the structure, the flow of a phrase. Think of literature, painting, or sculpture that you have loved and admire the similarities in form, grace, and style that you can see in your mind's eye in the way that this piece of music is put together. It has a liquid energy within it because it is *alive* in the moment that you are playing the notes, because the composer put a spark of his own genius into it that has survived long after he or she has left this earth, and because you are looking at a microcosm of a whole world of creative outpourings that have been humankind's gift back to the universe for all it has given us. Study one bar in detail and play that one measure alone until you *know* it. *Learn absolutely everything about that measure.* Not just the note values—learn the slurs, phrases, dynamic and expression markings, fermatas, mordents, and whatever else besides the actual notes. Feed all of that into your memory bank for that *one* measure. That is learning something *thoroughly*. That will give you confidence to learn the next measure. Then leave it alone— for an hour, a day, a week as you move on to the next bar, or phrase, or whole section.

This exercise will force you to **know** what notes you are "memorizing," and you will not be creating a separate action for the purpose of memorizing; you will just end up knowing those notes. As you do this, you may be surprised to discover that—even with a passage you can already play at speed—there are places in it where you do not know exactly what comes next *(because that pesky muscle memory had been substituting for actual knowledge!).* This is a great way to isolate these problem areas. Normally when we are learning or memorizing a piece of music, we may think that the whole piece, or the whole phrase, is difficult when, in fact, it is really only a few notes or bars that give us the trouble.

I know, I know—this morbidly slow process seems like it could take forever. Fortunately, it doesn't have to because you will, in a surprisingly short time, develop the intellectual habit of really looking at the notes you are playing the first time you see them and digesting what they have to tell you. *Close inspection* is what we are looking for. Don't *worry* about memory. If you investigate, meticulously, every note, every phrase, every measure in the piece as you learn to play it, you will end up knowing it from memory. As we have pointed out earlier: **what you *know*, you don't forget**.

I am confident that once you recognize that you are capable of *knowing thoroughly* even a small part of a larger work by the application of all of these tools in your mental-physical arsenal, you will realize that memorizing is not a separate, daunting task; it will become a natural consequence of your hard work and emerge as a surprise, perhaps, of its own accord as you continue to study the music. I know that it is not easy, but it is more dependable.

I, as a real-life example, am not a fast learner. I learn classical pieces very slowly by studying the notes minutely, as I want to understand how the composer created that sound. I really want to know. So, the learning process is filled with many "aha!" moments. By the time I have learned the notes, I have them memorized; it isn't *fast*, but it is also not a separate step.

Now is a good time to talk about the *speed* with which you are able to commit some music to memory. A lot of people are worried that they do not memorize information fast enough.

The Speed of Memorizing: *Damn the Torpedoes! Full Speed Ahead!*

Speed should not be a consideration when learning or memorizing a new piece of music. Instead, the emphasis should be on *thoroughness*. When you memorize something thoroughly, you will know it forever. It moves from your temporary memory to your lasting memory, and it becomes a part of your musical vocabulary. You still have to revisit it from time to time, but if you *truly* understand it, it will be easy to recover later on. When you are performing, no one in the audience knows what trials and tribulations you have gone through to come up with this enchanting, seemingly effortless rendition of the piece you are now presenting. And, of course, they shouldn't. It is human nature to strive for the best in oneself. So, you are bound to compare yourself to the best in the field.

But when you do that, you really don't have any idea what you are talking about.

Think about that—really. Nobody knows what goes on in the mind of another person: how they process information, what their emotional background is, how good they are at concentrating, what personal physical, psychological, or relationship challenges they may be experiencing, or what level of innate ability or emotional makeup they have. To this day, we have no accurate idea of how long it took Monet to paint *Water Lilies*, or Van

Gogh, *The Starry Night*, or how long it took Da Vinci to *not* finish the *Mona Lisa*. I wonder how many hours it took Michelangelo to sculpt *David*. Did he take breaks? Did he take days off? Did he work 20-hour days? Who knows? And, frankly, who cares? He ended up with *David*.

So how long, how many hours should you practice? The answer is: as long as it takes. We see, hear, and experience the *result* of the preparation, whether it be five minutes or five years.

And remember, when you are comparing yourself to others: there will always be someone who learns slower than you. And there will always be someone *younger and faster* than you. **(Unless, of course, your name is Yuja Wang.)**

Okay, so that's a joke—kind of.

With a true **knowledge** of all the notes you are playing, it will be much easier to

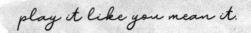

play it like you mean it.

Chapter 22

REPERTOIRE

"Play It Again, Sam..."

Well, *can* you play it again? You *could* three years ago. In order to "play it again," you have to *remember* and *rehearse* the song that you played for her five or 10 years ago. You need to have as much music as possible ready to play, not just as a professional cocktail pianist making a living playing requests but as a classical artist, a student, a friend, an amateur—a *pianist!*

Here is a bit of advice about developing your musical repertoire. Yes, this suggestion is coming from someone who learned this lesson the hard way. I dearly wish I had followed my own advice in my formative years. My repertoire would be three times as large as it is. Even today, I am guilty of these sorts of omissions. I have recorded over 375 pop songs on 30 albums, plus played another couple thousand or so over my 40-year career. In addition, I have recorded 15 or 20 pieces from the classical repertoire. Can I play all those today? Nope! I wish I could, but I can't. Try not to make that mistake.

Here is my suggestion.

Whatever music you are studying and actually preparing, up to the point of being performance-ready in recital, *keep playing them every so often for the next year, and the year after that, and so on.* Play them *all* every now and then. That way, six years later, you won't have to relearn them. That's how you develop a repertoire. You have *got* to have something to play on any occasion. And, if you intend to make music your profession, whether it be as a teacher or a performer or both, classical or pop—or both!—you need to have pieces of music at the ready at a moment's notice.

You will, of course, have your favorites, your go-to pieces—songs, ballads, novelty pieces, stunts, whatever that you love to play—your "signature" pieces. In other words, you don't need to keep up every single piece you ever learned, just the ones you love to play or that you know people want to hear. Think of what it is that you are trying to accomplish in the long run, career-wise or educationally, and galvanize your practice sessions into action toward that objective. Perhaps you have no idea yet what it is you intend to do with your music as you grow and mature. It is still a good rule to keep a memorized repertoire growing. There is no way that that cannot be a good thing. The important thing is that, as time goes by and you are preparing for the next recital, concert, or gig, you do *not* leave the earlier pieces behind.

This advice applies equally to classical and pop and from beginner to professional. It is just normally much easier to keep pop tunes in your head and fingers than it is the classical ones, for obvious reasons. With classical, of course, you have worked very hard to learn every note and play it properly, exactly like the printed page. With pop tunes, on the other hand, once you know the basic song, you can play it a hundred different ways.

Regardless of the type of music you are playing, **KEEP A LIST!** I can't stress that enough. If you don't, I guarantee (and I know from hard-won experience) that you will forget what you played two years ago. You must have a list to refer to. Think of it this way: if you are playing a song that is truly loved and timeless, like "All I Ask of You" from *Phantom*, it will be as beautiful and well-loved 20 years from now as it is today, 35 years after its debut—and very likely just as popular. Standards from the 1930s and '40s are just as popular with many listeners today as they were when they were first penned nearly a century ago. The same is true of the classics. Why does every student learn "Für Elise"? It is still played in concerts in hundreds of different arrangements by many combinations of instruments. It is just that good.

Of the 32 Beethoven sonatas, we mostly hear the *Pathétique*, the *Appassionata*, and above all, the *Moonlight* (the first movement). You probably learned "Clair de Lune" in middle or high school. It is one of the very few classical pieces that most nonclassical listeners can identify immediately and still want to hear. I still play it in concert. It is a perennial classic. Same with Rachmaninoff's "18th Variation."

And the same is true of the pop standards, like "Unforgettable," "Autumn Leaves," and a host of other titles that get rediscovered every 20 years or so.

You need tunes to play at the drop of a hat. Songs, classical pieces, whatever … *now* and later. Believe me, it will make your life so much more fun and stress-free. So next time you are at a party or some gathering where there is a piano, and someone asks you to play something, you can just say, "Sure." You don't have to hem and haw, think of what to play, wonder if you are going to mess up, or wonder what's appropriate—you will have a piece (or 10) prepared.

For casual gatherings, parties, social events, learn pieces that are *short*! Four minutes max. People want to hear you, but they don't want to listen "politely" or start to fidget; they want to be briefly entertained, and then they want to get back to chatting.

So, as you go through the next few (many!) years, have an ear out for something on piano that really grabs you, then obtain the sheet music, and start learning it. Or ask your teacher to help you learn it in addition to what you are already working on. Then learn it well and completely—no matter how long it takes—and play it over and over again for friends and at parties, and so on. You will be training yourself as not only a pianist but as an *entertainer*. You will be developing a repertoire that you will keep with you for the next 50 years.

I still get choked up when I remember the **first piece I ever performed** ("Dolly Dear").

I couldn't wait to get up onstage (the living room) and dazzle the crowd (all four of them—parents *and* grandparents) with my artistry! And dazzle 'em, I did! I remember reading the review some months later (when I had learned to read): "*A telling, impassioned performance of the candid, if somewhat obscurely poignant classic, 'Dolly Dear.'*" Come to think of it, it looked a lot like my mom's handwriting. Uncanny!

I know, I know—I'm bragging, but the point I am trying to make is I remember to this day how much I enjoyed that performance; and I am *pretty* sure that even today, I could perform it (all two notes!) at the drop of a …a…um…*extemporaneously!*

You get the idea. When you learn something, keep it in your mind and fingers. Many years later, you'll be glad you did.

Side note: Apropos the subject of **repertoire**, *I happen to love poetry. I have memorized many poems over the years, but I almost never have an opportunity to recite any of them.*

"Would you like to hear me recite a poem?"

"Gosh! I'd love to, but look at the time! I have to go get a root canal!"

Notwithstanding those accolades, I am sharing this personal tidbit for a reason. I cannot tell you how enjoyable—fulfilling!—it is to me to recite poems *to myself* when I am alone in my car, or at night when I can't sleep, or to just recite a poem quietly in my head while I am doing some mindless task, like taking out the garbage. They are my repertoire of the spoken word, and I rehearse them from time to time to keep them fresh. And I keep a list of the poems that I have committed to memory, so I don't forget one of them along the way.

Repertoire is something you always have with you. It enriches your life and makes your day more lovely. You have it when the lights go out, when you have to weather a storm (externally or internally), and when you are lonely or frustrated. It fuels your exhilaration when you are happy. It tugs viscerally at your heartstrings when you are sad; it fills your life with a beauty that only you know and can create at a moment's notice. It never leaves you.

But you must have it at your mental beck and call, or it can be frustrating when your heart wants to sing, but you forgot the words.

There is a beautiful sentiment that I would like to quote here from a writer named Arne Garborg:

"To love a person is to learn the song that is in their heart, and to sing it to them when they have forgotten."

Enchantingly expressed! You don't want to forget *their* song or the song that is in your *own* heart either. So rehearse it!

Another nuance: whatever you perform publicly, **your audience is more important than you.** It's all about them. So always notice their reactions and responses to *what* you play when you do perform. Notice that sometimes pieces, tunes, or songs that you do not think are particularly outstanding can be some of the audience's favorites. Make notes after every performance and keep them near the piano where you can review them from time to time. You may be truly surprised to find out which songs are requested over and over.

One of the things we all must watch out for is that our friends and fans will tell us only the good stuff. So be honest with yourself. *You* have to take that responsibility. Notice the responses honestly. Don't "lead the witness": "Did you like that last Bartók piece? Isn't 'Moon River' a great song?"

See, you can't convince a person to like what you like. But you *can* persuade most people to say something nice to make you feel good because most people are nice. So, learn to really listen to (or overhear) what they say, which pieces they mention the most, and which titles (that you really love and think you play exceptionally well) never get mentioned. Of course, everyone's taste is different; however, you will discover over time that some pieces in your repertoire consistently get a much better reception than others. That's why they become what are called "standards," new or old. Those are the ones you want to put on your "keep forever" list.

Now, go back to your music bookshelf, revisit some of those tunes you played a few years or months ago, and reminisce with yourself about how satisfying it was to play this piece or that; what a feeling of achievement it was to learn the Rachmaninoff *Prelude in C♯ Minor* or John Legend's "All of Me." Feel again the heartbreaking longing that you experienced learning the Brahms *B♭ Minor Intermezzo* or how you celebrated inwardly as you finally mastered the exquisitely crafted Chopin E♭ Nocturne and how you wish you had it in your fingers right now.

Visit again the great songs from musicals or pop music that you have seen or listened to. Relive the passion—*every single time you play it*—of "All I Ask of You"; the heart-wrenching feeling of nostalgia that resides within the fabric of a great movie theme like "Somewhere in Time" or "Out of Africa," both by the extraordinary composer, John Barry.

I think you will be surprised to find it easier to resurrect some of these beautiful pieces of music than you may have expected. And after you have reacquainted yourself with one of these gems, put the music where you can find it easily next week and the next and write its name down on your list. Over the next few months, watch that list grow and revel in the fact that you know *that* many tunes that you can play at a moment's notice whenever you feel the need to hear that melody and feel those exact keys under your fingers. Go and write down just *one* piece ***right now*** to put onto your "I must relearn this" list.

Happy hunting, and good luck!

Chapter 23

PLAYING BY EAR CAN'T BE LEARNED

"It Ain't Necessarily So"

This chapter assumes that, right now, you *can't* play by ear! You may be extremely gifted, well trained, and can play Chopin divinely but can't pick out a tune without the dots. It's not your fault. We weren't taught this mysterious skill that to some people comes naturally. So, it's time we changed all that. Become a triple threat: playing by ear, improvising, and arranging.

I personally know some very extraordinary classically trained pianists who can sit down and whip out a Beethoven sonata or two at a moment's notice but can't play a well-known tune at a party without the music. I was one of them. It's not our fault. I believed that myth so completely that I, like so many musicians, **never really tried**. This is much more common with highly trained, pedigreed classical musicians than with self-taught garage-band players. For one thing, if someone has never had lessons, they were never told they can't play by ear. So, they just figure it out.

Another nuance in this little game is that when a student is learning to read music, he is admonished by his teacher for trying to play the notes that *he heard his teacher play* rather than reading the music. This is an excellent and very justifiable reprimand because the point here is to *learn to read music*. The *error*, however, is to not treat "playing by ear" as a *separate and very valuable* skill that can be taught alongside the traditional musical education.

Before we embark on this subject, however, let's talk about why you should learn to play by ear in the first place. The truth is, there is no need to if you are quite content playing from the dots. Many fine artists spend their entire careers playing exclusively from the printed page. However, as this book is designed for the journeyman pianist, and not the concert artist, there is a good argument for learning to play by ear.

Let's look at a real-life scenario.

You are at a Christmas party. Among the guests are several accomplished, classically trained musicians. Time to sing some Christmas songs round the ol' upright.

"Would you be so kind as to play a few carols that we can all sing?"

"Well … um … no, not without the music" (blush). "How about something we can *all* do: a nice uplifting Gregorian chant?"

A sing along!

A cappella!

In Latin!

(all the music majors) **"YAY!"**

Remember, we are trying to change the basic premise, so I am looking at this facetiously, but from a purely analytical viewpoint, does that make any sense at all? This individual (you!) has just come from performing her senior recital at school in which she played the Schumann *Carnaval* brilliantly, and yet she cannot sit down and comfortably pick out a passable performance of "Winter Wonderland."

When I graduated from college in Texas, I had earned a degree in classical piano performance. I had no teaching qualifications and no interest in teaching. However, I needed a job. What could I do? Well, I knew a few pop standards by heart, and I had a large collection of books of pop tunes, mostly the old standards I grew up with. My dad loved Nat King Cole, Tony Bennett, the big bands, and yes, *Sing Along with Mitch,* and the Ray Conniff Singers, all of whom furnished me with an aural library of hundreds of tunes that I just sort of absorbed from the listening environment that my dad created for us. I had never *played* any of these *except with sheet music* at parties at the house—which happened often, since my mom loved hosting parties. So, naturally, when I went to get my first actual paid job in a sleazy nightclub, I couldn't play by ear. Instead, I brought along my 10 pounds of music books to the cocktail lounge.

Imagine this (fairly accurate) scenario:

"Can you play 'As Time Goes By?' "

"Sure! Just let me thumb through my *Complete Works of Everybody* collection and see if I have the notes. It's a really great tune, and I know you'll enjoy it. Is it really dark in here? Do you have a flashlight? It's here somewhere …"

"Never mind."

I didn't make a lot of tips.

Weaning Yourself from the Sheet Music

With that encouraging prologue, let's get started.

"Playing by ear can't be learned." I will let you in on a little secret. Let's keep this entre nous, please. "It ain't necessarily so." Simply put, playing by ear is a *skill*. And, as with any skill, it can be learned. Also, as with the acquiring of any skill, some people will be much better at it than others. People who can naturally play by ear, depending upon their skill at the instrument, can mimic what they have heard to a greater or lesser degree. For the rest of us who did not arrive on planet Earth prepackaged with that ability, there is hope in sight. I am here to tell you that the premise that "some can, some cannot" **is patently false.**

But isn't there "talent" or a "gift" involved too? You bet. Just like playing music exceptionally well from the *printed* page. People have different aptitudes, different cultural backgrounds, educations and, yes, inborn talents. That's just part of life. We are not all the same. But that doesn't mean we can't give things the ol' college try!

Itsty-Bitsy, Teenie Weenie Baby Steps

I am starting this discussion at an entry level, so please forgive me if I am telling you basics that you already know. I do want to communicate this information to musicians who are not familiar with the jargon and techniques of this mode of playing. I recognize that many of you have studied the piano in the traditional sense for years and are familiar with the language of classical music; however, in the hope that I can include *all* those people who want to teach themselves to play by ear, I will start at an entry point for someone who has very little knowledge of *nonclassical* musical terms.

The truth is you play by ear all the time. You read the notes, but as you read them, if you make an error, you correct it right away. So, all playing by ear is really doing is honing your natural aural acumen. As with everything else, it starts with *changing your mind about what you are capable of or "allowed" to do.*

Here's how:

To keep it simple—not *easy*, but simple—there are three ingredients that you need to master in order to play by ear: melody, harmony, and accompaniment style.

EXERCISES

Step One: A General Approach

When you begin playing by ear, you want to play an *approximation* of what you are hearing; it doesn't have to be note for note. Choose a song—and I do mean a "song," not a classical piece—that you are familiar with but have never played, one that you can hum, preferably a slow ballad, for obvious reasons.

Sing the first phrase of the tune and then find a note to start on—the one you were singing is fine. Any key will do, but you will probably find yourself defaulting to a key that you are comfortable with. That's okay. Key doesn't matter. Start picking out the single-note melody bit by bit, *by really carefully studying which way the melody goes.*

Start simply—does it go up or down? How far? One step? Two steps? An octave? You are just playing notes now, not making music. So, take your time and pay close attention to what the notes are doing. The goal of this exercise is to really grok *the way that melodies are made.* I mean that literally because when you examine a melody closely, you start to look for, and discover, repetitive patterns, trends, and characteristics that many popular melodies share. This is a journey of discovery, not an "I-hope-I-will-re-member-how-this-tune-goes." Most of us can *sing* a short melody on first hearing; why shouldn't you be able to *play* it? This exercise will help you to do just that: to get your fingers to do what your mind hears, right? When the notes go up an octave in your head, the finger knows to jump an octave on the keyboard. This will not happen at once, but as you examine the notes carefully, you will find that there is logic to the way melodies are constructed.

I feel that if you take one or two phrases of the song that you like and just imitate that part and play them over and over, you then start to see patterns emerge or idiomatic things that the composer has done, and I think you will be surprised that you can do more by ear than you thought. If there is anything in the way of *style* or *feel* that you can get from it, I encourage you to do so from the beginning. You may find that it is easier to imitate than you expected. Just the effort of trying to come up with the approximate notes is a very educational exercise, and you will very likely stumble upon techniques and devices of your own that you will put into your bag of piano tricks for use later on.

You want to admire the architecture, the practicality of how the melody goes away from its home base, goes on little adventures, and then comes back home at the end. This is why I want you to start with a familiar but noncomplex tune. Old standards are good for this exercise because so many of them are written in simple song form: A-A-B-A, where "A" is an eight-bar phrase that is then *repeated*. "B" is the contrasting "bridge" (the little adventure), and then "A" is restated (coming back home). You see, already this has become easier, as you only have *two* real melodies to pick out. It is patterns like these that you need to discover on your own through focused observation. It is far better to really "get" what is happening in *one easy tune* than to hunt and peck your way through dozens of melodies.

As with every endeavor, **genuine understanding** is the key to truly learning a subject. So, as you pick out your very first tune, examine it ever so closely, look for patterns, think of it as a puzzle that you are working out. Find out that it is not as complex as you first thought. As your focus increases, so do your accomplishments—small at first but growing until at some point you experience the "aha!" moments that are the milestones of learning any new subject. Along the way there will, no doubt, be obstacles, but you will get to a point where the whole pursuit is something you look forward to. You may even find yourself working out songs in your head when you should be paying attention to what your math teacher (or your wife!) is saying. Soon you will experience the feeling of confident anticipation of future achievement, morphing, at last, into one of pure joy! I promise.

Step One and a Half: Checking the Accuracy of the Melody

Buy the *original* published version of the sheet music to the song you have been experimenting with (not the "easy piano" version and not an arrangement). You want just the original piano, vocal, and chord symbols. Now, study, study, study! Look intently at the notes. See if what you picked out previously was correct, or nearly so. Sometimes what we sing back in our heads is slightly off because we hear it the way we *thought* we heard it the very first time all those years ago. I have been playing songs by ear for 50 years or so, but I still get the sheet music to a song that I am going to arrange and record because I want to know *exactly* what the composer meant before I make any changes. Sometimes a note or two in a melody makes the difference between a glorious tune and an ordinary one. So, look at the music carefully and make any corrections so that as you go forward, you will be on track.

Step Two: Harmony

With the sheet in front of you, read the notes, but don't necessarily *play* the notes. Just read them. But also look carefully at the chord symbols and start to figure out why *that* chord symbol means *those* notes. Do this meticulously! If you don't already know how to read chord symbols, get a chord symbol chart. You can easily download one. Just look for "chord symbols" and you will find everything you need. All you need to start with are major, minor, diminished and augmented triads and sevenths. A chord symbol chart will show you all of those shortcuts. At this point anything greater (ninths, 11ths, 13ths, suspensions, altered chords, and so on) should be ignored. Extended harmonies like those are more often used in jazz arrangements. For any chord *greater* than a seventh, for now, just substitute a seventh. *(Naturally, some won't sound right, but you are at the beginning of this exercise. So, get these basic chords into your brain, and you can go on from that secure foundation later on.)*

Determine what key you are in, and as you work your way measure by measure through the printed score, look closely at the chord symbol above that place in the score. Let's assume the chord symbol is F7 (F-A-C-Eb). Okay, that means an F-major triad with a minor seventh. The capital letter "F" denotes major, and the digit "7" denotes a *minor* seventh. Why does it denote a minor seventh? It just does. It's a convention; that's all. It is just a shortcut to those four notes. If you wanted a *major* seventh—E natural in this case—you'd have to say so: Fma7. In that case, once again, the capital letter "F" denotes a major triad, and the "ma" (in lower case) goes with the "7" to indicate a *major seventh*. Once you learn the shortcuts, the harmonic world is open to you. You can know with confidence that you just have to play some combination—*any combination*—of notes within that chord, and you will be okay.

So, now look at the accompanying notes on the printed page and notice that they are (usually, mostly) all notes that are contained within that chord. They could be arpeggiated, or stacked, or have any of the notes as the lowest, not just the root. The accompanying figure(s) could include some of the notes of the chord and leave out others. Really investigate; try to find out everything about that *one* chord.

Now would be a good time to memorize (with understanding) the notes of that one chord symbol, like Fma7. You undoubtedly know your triads and sevenths; you are probably familiar with their inversions. But even many schooled musicians are not familiar with these handy chord symbols that we are discussing, so this step is a very important one. Don't go past a chord symbol, at this stage, until you are sure you understand it completely. Remember, you are learning to wean yourself from the printed page. You are on your way to flying free on your brand-new musical wings, so keep in mind that you need to have a solid base to take off from! You are on a voyage of discovery.

So where are we? Let's take stock. We have started to pick out a one-line melody, and we have begun to decipher chord symbols. *I can't emphasize enough how important the learning of chord symbols is—**Very!** That's how!*

Continuing where we left off with chord symbols, it is time to purchase a "fake book," one that contains standards from the American songbook. For those of you who are not familiar with the term, a fake book is a collection of songs with only the melody line written out in notes in treble clef and the chord symbols placed above the notes where the harmony changes. No accompaniment is offered, just the one melody line.

Why is that? Because you *need* to know the exact notes of the melody (even if you change them later on), but you do *not need* to know the exact notes of the accompaniment. The fake book provides the essentials, the melody and the harmonic changes. You are "faking" the rest, inventing as you go along, having been provided with the basic road map. You, the artist, are invited to create the rest of the performance according to your own musical tastes and abilities. That is how a group of musicians who have never met can all jam together. They can achieve this as long as they have the same "chart" (another word for "fake" sheet music).

By far the longest term of your internship will be to learn to read these charts. They are the map to destinations; you choose the route. Early in your study, you will play rather simple versions of the song in front of you, just getting used to reading the chord symbols quickly enough to play the tune at tempo. As your ability increases, you will find that you are able to get a little more creative with the left-hand patterns. You might start out accompanying with block chords, then switch to an arpeggiated accompaniment, and from there, move to alternate patterns that complement the melody. Look at arpeggios as broken chords, which they are. Then realize that, as long as you play the notes of a chord *somehow or other,* you will be playing that harmony.

Try spacing out the chord with both hands, or try it in different registers, till you hear something you like. Listen to guitar strumming, in folk music, for example. This ability develops, over time, into what is called arranging. I have found over the years that much of my stylistic approach to accompanying a melody has been inspired by, or learned from, classical music. You absorb what the great composers did and follow, imitate, or emulate those idiomatic sequences and configurations of notes. One great source of inspiration can be found in the art songs of Schubert and Schumann; for in those, the piano part is a de facto accompaniment, albeit a very sophisticated one.

Okay, so we are at a point in this cognitive process where we are moving over from reading the printed sheet music note for note, to something of a hybrid—a musical halfway house, if you will—which is the reading of a fake chart. So become really good at using this wonderful tool because it is a vital step in your journey to musical freedom.

Step Two and a Half: Harmonic Choices

This is the part where you learn *which* chords to play under a given melody. This is a lifetime study, so don't expect to arrive at this in a few weeks. However, here are some shortcuts gleaned from my personal trials and tribulations that will hopefully shorten your term of apprenticeship.

By the time you have reached this step, you will have familiarized yourself with the jargon of how the *color* of chords are denoted in chord symbols (major, minor, diminished, augmented). Now is the time to investigate just where the harmonies change *under* the melody. We can all hear where a chord needs to change to a different one. So, take this time to work out for yourself just how this magic happens. You will notice at once that there are four primary chords that get used over and over. You probably already know this, so I'll be brief. They are the I, IV, V and VI chords in any key. In the key of C, for example, that would be C, F, G, and A minor. With this knowledge at your fingertips (pardon the metaphor), start noticing patterns and conventions—e.g., chords very often change from a I chord to a VI, to a IV chord, to a V chord, and back to a I. An easy-to-recognize example of this chord progression can be found in the tune "Heart and Soul" that we all pick out on the piano at an early stage in our playing. You would immediately recognize the usual three-hand version, in which the person playing the accompaniment (with two hands) is playing the aforementioned chord sequence and the person up top is banging out the (one-handed) melody.

Side note: When picking out a song without the music, if you are not certain what key the song you are playing is in, go to the end. The song will conclude, normally, on a I chord, which makes us feel satisfied and comfortably "at home." That I chord, is, of course, the key the song is in.

Watch, study, examine, and be meticulous in your search, reminding yourself that you will figure out this brainteaser because the reward at the end is independence from the printed page.

You might try this with a simple folk song like "Leaving on a Jet Plane" by John Denver. Learn to play the one-note melody and then just **guess**, amongst those chords, which one is appropriate. I am willing to bet that you will get it right on the first try. From then on, it's trial and error to get you to the next chord change, but your "trial" will become more and more accurate and consistent, and your "error," less frequent.

To reiterate: We have the four colors of chords (major, minor, diminished, augmented), and we know how to build triads and seventh chords. So, use those basic harmonies as a base from which to move forward. Those four chords (I, VI, IV, and V) and their four colors are your rock, your lifeline to harmonizing a tune. There are, of course, extended harmonies, but don't be put off by complex chord symbols. They are nothing more than patterns you do not yet know. They will come later. You can easily find them in the books on spelling chords. We are at an entry point, and I don't want you to get overwhelmed at the start.

Step Four (of Three Steps): Accompaniment Ideas

Now that we have touched upon harmonizing a melody, let's look at stylistic ideas. This is the next step to playing by ear. You can't just suddenly manufacture a style of playing that is unique to you. You learn a great deal from how others have solved a musical problem.

For this exercise, play the tune from the printed page. We mentioned above that we want to learn the exact notes of the melody from the original. That said, the admonition about accuracy applies to the *melody* only. As for the accompaniment, don't be stuck to the notes on the page. They are not inviolable. They are a *suggestion* of how to play the basic tune. Many times, a player who reads will play the exact notes of the accompanying figure on the printed page as though that were the only way to play it.

That is not the case. When sheet music is published, transcribers are hired to put the notes down on paper. The transcriber puts down her own view of how best to communicate the feeling of the original artist-recorded version so that you, the musician, can recreate it in a satisfying way. These transcribers are very skilled craftsmen, and there is a lot to be learned from what they write down. However, what they submit is their *interpretation*; often, it is a piano reduction from a band performance. As we go forward, you will see that if you don't like something about the accompaniment, you can change it. This is not Beethoven. Every artist makes changes to his liking. The sheet is only a map, a starting point.

At this point in your learning, what you want to get from the printed page is an overview of the *different ways of accompanying a melody.* We will often find that for a certain song, there is an idiomatic rhythmic figure or a defining recurring accent, things like that. These patterns or sequences will come to life off the printed page as a reward earned from your close observation. Remember that you are solving a puzzle. When you play the song from the sheet, don't just play the notes willy-nilly, without understanding. This is an exercise in *comprehension*.

The reason that you are digesting these musical directions for future use is for when it becomes time for you to play songs in your own personalized style. Did they arpeggiate the accompaniment? Were there lots of repeated chords? What rhythmic patterns do you notice? On and on, looking for clues. "So *that's* how he made that sound!"

It's really fun to discover how a particularly distinctive musical feature was created. Yes, at this point, look at all the minutiae. Now is the time for in-depth study. Once you have a basic understanding of how it's done, I encourage you to continue your self-education the way I did; play through hundreds of songs, both with the complete sheet music and also with just the fake charts, and keep experimenting with different accompaniment styles, keys, and variations on the existing melody.

Later on, when you are comfortably playing by ear, you won't be doing this; however, these devices, methods, techniques, and recurring sequences will have become a part of your musical vocabulary and will serve you well when you are arranging songs as you are evolving your own personal style.

So, there you have it—the entry hall, as it were, to the kingdom of musical sovereignty. In time you will have explored all the many architectural features, the interior design and structure, and the tapestries that adorn the walls, so that at the culmination of all your concerted efforts and exhaustive study, you will shed your technical crutches altogether and declare your musical autonomy. You have built for yourself a solid foundation upon which to construct a vehicle for expression of the music that is within you, waiting for its moment to shine forth and illumine the world around you.

Now, soaring free of the shackles that for so long bound you to the printed page, let's proceed to the next logical step.

Chapter 24

IMPROVISATION

Stream of Consciousness or ADD?
Who Cares?

This chapter, as in every chapter, is about putting a new lens on your thinking. If you have never improvised anything and have always played only the notes on the page, if you think you can't play by ear or improvise over a melody that you already know, then this discussion should be a helpful one.

I am not going to delve into the specific techniques of musical improvisation; rather I want to give you some insight into how to approach the task at hand from a philosophical perspective. There are numerous great texts out there that examine and teach methods and skills that are very helpful in freeing you completely from the printed page. I encourage you to do some research and find one, or several, that resonate with your personal learning style.

Here, however, I want to discuss the subject of improvisation as a *concept*. Throughout this book, I have tried to help you make changes in your playing by changing your *mind*, not by changing the way you push the keys. So, let's briefly touch on a spurious consideration about improvisation that we may have picked up along the way in our musical education. And that is, once again, an assertion we have all heard made casually by very knowledgeable, well-schooled musicians.

"Improvisation is something that jazz musicians do. I am a classical pianist, not a jazz player; ergo, I do not improvise." (Even though we know that historically, all the great classical composers were also great improvisors. That skill, in the classical field, has fallen away in the past hundred years or so. I have no idea why, but it mostly has.) Let's address *that* one right now.

Musical Improvisation Is What Thoughts Sound Like

Do you wish you could improvise something wonderful, but you don't know where to start? Tell me about it. I mean, actually—**right now**—start talking about why it is you can't seem to improvise, or why you would like to be better at it, or what you don't understand about improvisation—whatever thoughts you have about it. Just stop reading for a few minutes and talk about them—**out loud**. Tell me, or a friend, all the many thoughts you have on the subject. Try to express your frustration with it in as many ways as you can—how the subject fascinates you, how it eludes your best efforts, or how you love to do it but don't feel expert at it. Go on, rant, vent, discuss, rhapsodize, and try to say what you have to say any way you can. Keep talking until you have said everything you can think of on the subject.

Take a breath.

Guess what?

You just improvised.

The Mind at Play

What is improvisation from a holistic view? It is following your mind's ramblings—you just need a good segue from thought to thought. Improvising is the art of *listening* to your mind's meanderings and translating those thoughts into sound.

It is letting your mind wander off into variations of expression while adhering to the subject at hand. Or not. It is the same thing as talking with a friend. When you start a conversation about something that deeply interests both of you, you don't plan out everything you are going to say; you just start talking. The two of you create together a conversation that has never before seen the light of day. You have an anecdote to tell. You don't just tell it once; you say it a dozen different ways. You elaborate. If you happen to say something you really liked the sound of—maybe an elegant or clever turn of phrase—you might want to say it again to emphasize your point. You may even want to memorize it because it was so clever! You could quote yourself later! That is improv. We all do it.

When improvising, here are some things to think about. Naturally, the more piano technique you have, the better you will be able to "say" those ideas that pop into your head. That's pretty much a no-brainer. It's the same with speaking; the greater your vocabulary, the more books you have read, and the greater your fluency with the language, the better you will be at relating a humorous or dramatic story.

You see, many times when someone is new at improvising, he just sits down at the piano with no plan or even an idea of where to begin. None! He just starts pushing the keys, willy-nilly, makes a few unpleasant sounds, and gets frustrated or loses interest because he is not following any actual musical or mental direction. Maybe he is trying to sound like a jazz player he admires. Maybe he hopes to write a truly beautiful melody but falls short of his own (vague) expectations.

Okay. Listen up.

In order to improvise, you have to *find out who you really are*. Now, I know that is the crucial question of the ages, and I am not attempting to answer what Hume, Balzac, and Kant *can't!* But I do have a knack for dumbing things down for myself so that I can grasp a complex idea in a simple way. If you want to discover who you really are, it is quite straightforward: **look at yourself**. Step outside of your body and mind for a while and have a look at yourself. Watch what you DO.

To get you going on this path to self-discovery, here are some questions. Answer them (to yourself) honestly. Not what *should be* the answer or you *wish* were the answer—just the candid response. If you are not sure, then just look at what sort of behavior you default to when left alone with no one else in the room. And inspect *that*.

Here we go:

- What's the first thing you do when you get up in the morning? Shower? Coffee? Read your email?

- What sort of clothes do you like to wear? Loud colors/Muted pastels?

- Are you an extrovert or an introvert?

- What genres of books do you read? Dramas? Comedies? Classics? Comic books?

- How do you talk to others? Do you do all the talking? Are you a good listener?

- Are you animated, with lots of hand motions when you talk?

- Do you love the outdoors?

- Do you like a rainy day? Or love the sunshine?

- Would you prefer to sit quietly by yourself than to be with other people?

- What makes you happiest?

- What gives you a feeling of achievement?

- Are you energetic or sedentary?

- Do you like poetry? Hate poetry?

- Which do you prefer? Jackson Pollock or Raphael?

- Do you argue a lot? How do you handle someone who yells at you?

- Do you multitask? Do you do five things at once? Or do you focus intently on one action?

You can go on with this exercise as long as you like, but the point is to get you to *actually examine yourself* to find your default place, your comfort zone, where you spend your mental and spiritual time *without any judgment at all.* Hopefully, you will discover something about yourself—philosophically—that brings you to a realization about what you truly believe in. You are always looking for that moment of "Ah! *That's* what I actually want to express with my music!" Something like that.

As you do this you will find that—if you are honest with yourself—you will see who you really are by how you approach situations in your life. Not how you *wish* you were, but how you actually respond to the rewards, the challenges, the everyday mundane actions like taking out the garbage. Are you cheerful when you do that? Indifferent? Annoyed?

OK, you get the premise. So how does that translate into improvising music at the piano? Here are some tips.

When you sit down at an unfamiliar piano for the first time, to hear its voice, feel what it can do, and so on (*with no one listening to you!*) where do you put your hands without thinking? The middle of the keyboard? Treble? Bass? Do you play in keys that have lots of sharps or flats? Major? Minor? Lots of chords? Single lines? Gently? Rough? Do you start with a bass line? A high treble to hear the upper end voice of the instrument?

Can you see how these *impulses* are a glimpse into **who you are** and what you believe about yourself? Do you play quietly and pensively? Loudly and boisterously? Somewhere in between? You can see where I am going with this.

You know how to play the piano. Now, you have observed yourself in life enough to get a pretty good idea of who you are, philosophically. You might tell an intimate friend what you have discovered about yourself. You might be eloquent when you do that. You might whisper it as a secret between the two of you. Now it is time to express yourself in this *other language* that you have at your disposal.

EXERCISES

Let's start to play something.

1. Start with a tonic chord in the left hand in the key of C. Just a triad, or maybe add a sixth for interest (C-E-G-A), or another key that you have chosen. Just hold the chord or play it over and over. Play it as a block chord, then arpeggiate it; maybe play it with a different note in the bottom (inversion) and establish that harmony fairly well in your ear. Don't even worry about rhythm at this point. You are just establishing a bed of sound over which to let your mind wander. At this point, just play this one chord.

2. Now start the right hand wandering. Begin on the tonic of that chord and move using the notes of that major scale, up a few, back down, around, this way and that. Listen to what you are doing and be comfortable with the exercise, not so much how it sounds as just noticing what you naturally do (hint: it's okay if it sucks). Do you like flowing melodies? Angular? Startling? Classical sounding? Smooth movement? Big jumps? Notice what pleases your ear and do more of that.

3. Try the same exercise in minor. I usually default to a Gm9 harmony (G-Bb-D-F-A♮) because it seems to let my mind get going easily. I usually start with a 10th in the left hand, G-D-Bb, and A-D-A in

the right hand. To my ear, that minor ninth harmony has a bit of longing built into it. But you see, that is a part of who I am musically. That sound resonates with me on a deeply personal level. Why? I don't know. It just does, so it is a starting point for me.

4. Once you have done this for a while, find a familiar tune, one that you can play by ear, or memory, and play it with one hand. Then start changing a note or two, maybe embellishing the phrase to your liking. You see, the only way to become a great improvisor is to improvise a lot.

5. Most jazz improvisation is done over the chord changes of a particular song. So, what you do now, in this next part of your study, is to take a familiar song, using only the fake chart, and play it as written. Then—slowly!—change your melodic line according to the chord changes. In other words, if the chord is a C-major chord, play other notes of the C-major scale, while using the existing melody of the song as a *guide* to depart from and return to. When it changes to another chord, you change, too, segueing into the next harmony in a way that appeals to you, then using the scale notes inherent in *that* chord, and so on. As you do this exercise, you can get farther and farther away from the original melody, but you—having the melody in your head—will want to return to it every few notes or measures, in order to let the listener (you, in this case) recognize what the tune actually is.

Back to the metaphor of telling a story—tell us the melody, then say something about it that interests you. Maybe you will highlight a particularly interesting phrase or a sudden chord change in the original (a surprising turn in the evolution of the story). Maybe you like a little motif so much that you use it over and over and then vary *it* to your liking. Think in metaphorical, philosophical terms because that will continually take you back to who you are musically. Above all, *enjoy* these musical excursions, ongoing journeys of personal exploration.

With any luck, you will find out things about yourself in your life *away* from the piano. Maybe the piano (in this experiment) is just a tool for self-discovery. Always allow for the possibility of new revelations that you never planned for. Perhaps you will finally realize that you never wanted to improvise in the first place, and you just thought you did or should. Here, it's about the journey, not the destination. Trite, but true. It's about the joy of knowing more about yourself every day. Maybe the piano is just a laboratory in which you perform experiments that help you to recognize what you truly love, and you continue to blossom into more of who you believe yourself to be. The final outcome—to improvise or not to improvise—is not important. What *is* important is that because you have this set of skills that allows you to play the piano the way you do, you have at your disposal, any time you like, a physical device upon which to play out and explore the ever-changing, ephemeral world of "who am I right now?" and that could be different today from how it will be tomorrow.

I have always felt that the way that I choose to express myself at the piano tells people a lot about who I am. Maybe it does, maybe not; but for me, as I watch and listen to what I play on this marvelous instrument, there are moments when I say to myself, *"Now **that** is who I really am!"* I am being literal here. It's a wonderful feeling, being true to yourself, isn't it? Well, you have this incredible man-made device that is a window to your soul, one that, through the simple act of pushing keys, first randomly, then with a purpose, can illumine secret places in your mind that you may otherwise have never visited. That is, of course, what all art is for, and why we *"have"* to do it.

Music—itself—doesn't even have physical substance. It is a link between the material world and the ethereal realm that exists only in thought and emotion. We are fortunate indeed to have the piano to serve as a conduit through which we can share the beauty of our own universe with the rest of the world. In the end, improvisation is conversing at the piano and telling the listeners, "This is what I believe." All art, to me, is just the invisible spirit made visible.

So here we are again at the baby-steps point of improvisation. But, hope-fully, by now you will have overcome any fear you have of approaching this "unknowable" subject, for that is the key. When you unlock that door, there is another door and another, till you stand at the base of a majestic mountain range of unlimited possibilities stretching to the horizon. With each step in the direction of heightened self-awareness, you will be bet-ter able to

play it like you mean it.

Chapter 25

ARRANGING

Nice Window Treatments!

Now that we have dipped our toes into the refreshing waters of improvisation, the next logical step is to wade out a little deeper into the discovery of our musical selves by arranging an entire song.

It is not as hard as you think to step away from the dots and play *your* version of your favorite song. An entire library of books has been written about arranging music at the piano, so there are numerous references to help the student arranger. However, in this book, as I have done throughout, I wish to approach the subject from a philosophical perspective. I want to share my ideas on the state of mind and the emotion whence the arrangement actually has its genesis, a discussion of "where do we come from emotionally, narratively, philosophically?" about putting one's own signature on someone else's song.

Let's take a global look at arranging, and then you will take it from there according to your musical knowledge, skills, ideas, and most of all, your musical tastes.

My philosophy has been to try to thoroughly *entertain* an audience of "normal" (i.e., *nonmusically trained)* people with high quality music. I try to do whatever is necessary at the keyboard to create the effect I want, whether the technique is kosher or not. I love inner voice movement, hemiola, countermelody, and lots of cross rhythms. That said, I try not to impose my musical tastes on my listeners. If I find out (through observation) that a sequence of notes that I find simply divine doesn't do anything for the listener, I try to change it in some way while still retaining my artistic integrity because onstage, and recording, I am playing for *them*, not *me*. So that consideration is always first and foremost. Some of you may disagree with that premise, but that is the beauty with arranging. You put your unique viewpoint onto the song. Everyone is different.

People often ask me what my musical influences are and where I draw my inspiration from when I am arranging a song for piano solo. Well, there are three composers to whom I turn most often, musically and aesthetically, whose styles have become such a part of my musical thinking that I don't think about them when I am writing an arrangement, but their genius lives somewhere in my subconscious and resonates with my musical viewpoint.

Because it may be helpful to those of you who are starting your journey in arranging, I will include some specific examples of how these particular composers have contributed to my musical approach. So, who are these three great geniuses? They are **Debussy, Chopin, and Rachmaninoff.**

Debussy

In the music of **Debussy**, and the whole genre of impressionism, one creates a mood, a backdrop, a diaphanous curtain through which to view the subject in the distance, as it were. An *impression* of the thing, rather than the thing itself. It is not a photographic likeness of an object or a person but a pastel hint that lets you know exactly what it is without saying so. The colors and lines are a little indistinct, and the whole composition makes you *feel* the environment in which the melody lives.

Have a listen to Debussy's *Reflections in the Water*, or *Sunken Cathedral*, and then to my arrangement of the beautiful crossover country song "Snowbird" in which I used impressionistic "sound painting" inspired by the style of Debussy. Another example of that style of arrangement can be heard in the introductory bars of my take on "When You Wish Upon a Star."

Chopin

In the music of **Chopin**, there is an elegance and lacelike delicacy in his melodic embellishments and scale passages. He has a seemingly unending supply of musical ideas with which to ornament a simple tune. He goes on forever. A perfect example of that is his *Berceuse* (lullaby). You can hear my interpretation of that small masterpiece on my album entitled *Chopin*. If you listen carefully, you will hear that the left hand is playing the exact same one-bar figure over and over throughout the entire piece while the right hand starts with a simple melody and then goes into rhapsodies of variations, all over that one accompaniment figure. True genius.

I have been inspired by that master to make use of extended embellishments. A good example is in the first iteration of the Gershwin song "Maybe" on my *Rhapsody in Blue* album. In this case, the embellishments are more prominent than the actual simple melody. As an artistic choice, you may or may not agree with it, but it is a good example of my adapting and using a musical device that I admire in my own arrangement of a song, removed by about a century from the source of inspiration.

Now notice in my arrangement of "Baby Mine," from the movie *Dumbo*, the use of the left-hand figure throughout. I modeled this after the *Berceuse*, with embellishments inspired by that wonderful lullaby. I also used that left-hand ostinato technique again in an arrangement of the Christmas song "Away in a Manger" from my CD entitled *Do You Hear What I Hear?* Both arrangements were inspired by—not copied from—that beautifully crafted masterpiece.

Rachmaninoff

When you think of **Rachmaninoff**, you think of power, strength, and impassioned musical statements. Yes, often dark and serious. In fact, that "darkness" translates into drama and intensity in the listener's world. Those same qualities give a sense of suspense, building up to the climactic finale of a phrase or an entire piece of music. I have tried to infuse into many of my arrangements some of that signature power, that "one-more-time-with-feeling" emotional outpouring that is a seminal ingredient in so much of his music. You can hear my adaptation of that style in the interlude of my arrangement of "All I Ask of You" from *Phantom,* which drives the listener forward from the first time through the song into the second passionate utterance of that captivating melody.

The Path to Self-Expression: Who Do They Think I Am, Anyway? Tell Them!

No two of us, reading the same piece of sheet music for the first time, will play it identically. We will—unconsciously—imbue it, even at the early stages of learning the notes, with our own musical conception of what is appropriate and with our own way of touching the keys, feeling the tempo and rhythm. Which means that whenever we, as pianists, play a new song, we instinctively play it in a way that resonates with our own musical philosophy. Suppose you asked Rembrandt and Chagall each to draw a horse. We all know how different these two expressions would be. Each artist's work is the product of his own cultural background and history, abilities, likes, and dislikes. In a word, he comes from who he *is* and, in that way, shapes his identity as an artist.

I am often asked what prompts me to write an arrangement the way that I do. The short answer is that it is who I *am* that directs me. So how do you find out who you *are* musically in case you are not sure from the start? The above exercises are an entrance point. Yet with a highly subjective topic like this, it helps to approach the discussion of it from different viewpoints in the hope that we strike a (metaphorical) chord that speaks to your understanding.

Music is a moving, breathing art, very much alive. I compare my arranging approach to that of speaking, or the act of painting, or of sculpting—by which I mean I am molding the work as I play. Therefore, there is a lot of *rubato*, ebb and flow, give and take, dynamics of loud and soft. When you play the piano, the listener is witnessing the actual act of creation. Worlds and swirls of sounds are happening as your mind goes through its mental and emotional musings till you find the "right" destination for that particular phrase. When you begin to arrange a piece of music, and you have a blank slate in front of you, where do you start? Don't just get a book on arranging and start trying some of the instructive (albeit probably very worthwhile) exercises.

Just think, when you—or someone else—are telling a story, your voice is not monotone nor does it come across in a metronomic rhythm. You use inflection, varied speed, highs and lows, and your volume and level of enthusiasm change as you go. Sometimes you stop and think of a comment in a sort of parenthetical way; you pause, go to that thought, express it, or at least refer to it, and then come back to the main idea. Well, arranging is no different. It is a language replete with punctuation, inner meanings, subtleties, and parenthetical comments interspersed within a phrase.

What one normally does in an arrangement is to quote the tune accurately up front so that the listener knows what we are talking about. You need to know where you are coming *from* before you decide where you are going *to*. That said, once you are really familiar with the tune, you can start your adventure. If you are a player who is used to playing the exact notes on the page, then this is a good time to begin to wean yourself from the dots.

The Prodigal Song

Let the song go away from you, maybe get into mischief, play some clams, gamble away the family fortune, fall into musical ditches, dust itself off, and do some more wandering, till at the end of the day, having got those meanderings out of its system, it comes back to your open arms, ready to be welcomed home warmly so that it can start to follow your—now experienced—direction. Think of starting to arrange as "the mind at play." Follow your thoughts as they jump—sometimes abruptly—from idea to idea, topic to topic, musical phrase to musical phrase.

Start with a ballad, something slow and not technically demanding. Again, *think about who you are:* your personality, your likes and dislikes, certainly your *musical* tastes, what styles of music you are drawn to, what songs make your heart soar, and what artists move you. Try to discover *why* their communication does that for you. In the fine arts, do you prefer representational painting, architecture, and sculpture? Impressionistic? Abstract? Mythical? Sci-fi? Just let your mind go! *Be free! Soar, like Icarus! Fly away! Fly away!! (Just remember to come back before dinner! And before your wings melt!)*

If you find that a difficult exercise, and you just don't know who you "are" yet, aesthetically speaking, then refer back to the exercise in the previous chapter and begin by taking one phrase of a ballad and changing it ever so slightly. Just change a note or two of the melody to give it an embellishment, just a note up a half step and back to the original note or up a few scale notes and back. You will likely come back to the original because it sounds the best. That is okay. What I want you to realize is that you have every right to deviate from the printed page, and nothing terrible *(but maybe something wonderful!)* will happen. Just because the publisher printed it that way does not mean it is sacrosanct. You are **freeing your mind**, which is the first step toward learning any new discipline or skill—knowing that it is *okay to do it* and *then* acquiring the skills to perfect it.

This is also a great time to remember to give yourself all the freedom you need to make awful sounds, "to boldly *(badly?)* go where no one has gone before." Don't be afraid to hit lots and lots of sour notes; that's the learning process. As you experiment, probably keep a tape running, so you can recreate a set of notes or a phrase that you like. I use my iPhone. You may surprise yourself with what you can do. The best practice, in my experience, is finding a song that I already know and love and then playing it over and over and over—and over!—trying out different tempos, rhythms, or dynamics. Try an Edith Piaf torch song in a rhumba style or an up-tempo standard like "New York, New York" as a sultry ballad. Anything goes! At any level of playing, you can experiment—don't be afraid of hitting sour notes—just try something you have never tried before. It doesn't have to be difficult or technically demanding, just a little turn of phrase. Try drastically changing a note or two of the melody line just because you feel like it. Do not be afraid of sounding awful or stupid. I can tell you from long years of experience that I have sounded *very stupid* on numerous occasions while on my way to finding something sublime—many times through sheer chance or by making one more mistake that yielded a brand-new idea.

As you do this, you will also find out what your natural instincts are. Do you (by default) play a lot of embellishments? Do you instead remove some notes and want to hear a sparser sound? Do you find yourself drawn to particular chord voicings? Maybe you gravitate toward a particular key that is easier for you or just sounds better. You do not have to play the song in the original key. The original key was perfect for that artist. But you will find out that playing a song in many different keys will impart a different feel, or ambiance, to the song. I play through a new song in many keys till I find the right one for me to express my voice. I almost always find that once I change keys *by a lot*, say a major third or even a fifth away from the original, that I suddenly have brand-new ideas for interpretation, even if I then go back to the original. Don't be afraid to play the song in a key that doesn't suit it at all. This is an experiment. You will make new discoveries about the song and about yourself till you find the exact place where that song and your portrayal of it "need to live" on the keyboard. A song that sounds bland in the middle register of the piano can come to life when moved up a few steps. Try it.

Maybe you have fluid arpeggios in your arsenal; maybe your specialty is embellishments, and on and on. Discover your strengths. Maybe certain accompaniment styles fall under the hand more naturally. All of these features of your natural abilities come together to eventually blossom into the arranger that you will become. Experiment to find out what sounds and feels "satisfying" to you.

Musical fulfillment is, to me, an all-important—and compelling—factor in my arrangement of a tune. It is hard to define, but we know how it feels. Let's investigate it in more detail.

Putting It All Together

When I am starting an arrangement from scratch, there are some general elements that I usually try to incorporate into my arranging process. Thus, we will start with a summary description of the goal we are trying to accomplish and then go into specifics. Finally, we will discuss in depth one of my most successful arrangements as a real-world example of a how I craft a musical tale. Here we go.

What Are You Trying to Say? The General Thrust of an Arrangement

First of all, you go about engaging the listener's attention, and then you *hold* it through your musical peregrinations until you come to the satisfying conclusion of your musical story. The listener feels complete and fulfilled. It is not a style nor a certain use of arpeggios, trills, harmonies, or other techniques. Rather, it is a **musical storyline** that is *rewarding* in that it gives you a starting point. It progresses through a musical voyage, possibly with some surprising twists and turns, holds your interest through-

Play It Like You Mean It

out because it makes logical sense in the vignette you are creating, makes you eager to know the conclusion of the story, and then brings the entire adventure to a thrilling—or perhaps very gentle—denouement. It makes *sense*. Like a four-course dinner.

Now for some specifics.

The Hors D'Oeuvre: Foie Gras

You don't have to start with the actual opening bars of the song. But you *do* want to engage your listeners' attention at once and not lose it before the familiar part of the song begins. Let them know what you are about to say. Certainly, you can play an extended introduction. But make sure it has something to do with the overall mood. Actually give the opening bars some careful consideration. First impressions and all that. An assertive, dramatic rhythmic opening can tell you immediately what the song is about. Michael Jackson's songs do this gorgeously. Listen to the opening bars of "Billie Jean" or "Bad." They grab you immediately.

If, on the other hand, you want to head right into the substance of the song, then by all means, make it memorable. Look to the greatest examples of that sort of "dive-right-in" approach. These include the opening four notes of Beethoven's Fifth Symphony or the opening bars of Liszt's Second Hungarian Rhapsody. On the flip side of that sort of startling announcement are the dulcet opening Db-major thirds of Debussy's "Clair de Lune," which take you at once into the realm he wants you to live in for the duration of the whole piece. (*I always choose the very finest examples of a stylistic technique to give myself ideas.*)

Use your opening to create an instant mood, and then (at least in most three or four-minute songs) you will probably keep the character of that mood throughout. The opening notes can really make the listeners decide whether they want to hear more or not, especially in these short-attention-span times. So make the initial sounds count.

The Main Course: Roast Pheasant in Wine Sauce

So, now that you have introduced the subject at hand, don't betray the listener. You said, "This is what this story is about." **Now tell it to them.** This is the substance of the arrangement, the meat or fish. This is where you inject your personality into the telling of the tale. How would *you* tell this story? What is an arrangement *for*, anyway? Well, the reason you are doing an arrangement in the first place is that you feel that you have something to comment about the song. Perhaps you have a slightly different view from that of the versions you have heard. Perhaps your take on this lovely melody will introduce it to people who would otherwise never have listened to it. Some people want to hear every version of their favorite song that they can find. You need to have a *reason* to arrange the song.

The Side Dish: Cider-Glazed Brussels Sprouts and Bacon

Here is an approach: after you have played or stated a phrase of the actual song, stop a minute and see if you have something to say about what you just played. Maybe you make a musical "comment" about it and then go on. It is as if you are relating an interesting anecdote about a real-life story. The simple statement could be "Yesterday we went to the beach." The comment is *"I love the beach. It always lifts my spirit; often when I am there, I just stare out into the ocean and feel the vastness of the universe, and it makes me want to dance!"* Then on to the next actual sentence, "We stayed there all day." The next comment is *"The delicious minutes relaxed into carefree hours. The hours transformed into a reposeful day, and before we knew it, it was time to wave goodbye to the beach even though we wished it could last forever."* And so on.

The Palate Cleanser: Lemon Sorbet

You may, while relating an anecdote, occasionally pause for a moment or two to let the listener reflect on what you just said. Just so with a musical statement. Silence is golden. Short phrases, longer pauses, the judicious employment of silences—these are all part of communication. Let your imagination soar and try not to put constraints on your creative juices. Don't make the mistake of censoring your ideas because they seem "dumb," too far away from the original, or not in the character of the song. Remember, you are an arranger at this point, so go ahead—*arrange!*

The Dessert: Chocolate Mousse and the After-Dinner Cordial

So now, you have said what you had to say. You have displayed this little gem in its original simplicity; you have shared your musings about it and allowed it to open its petals so people can see deep inside its heart. It is now time to say goodbye to the listener. And as a farewell gesture, here is a gentle reminder of the opening musical motif as the curtain closes on this little vignette. So here, *once again*, is a statement of the melody that inspired this arrangement in the first place. There is a time during this procedure that one says to oneself, *"Yes! That's what I meant to say!"* Then you recognize that it is time to leave it alone and release it into the universe. So, there you have it, some general thoughts on the subject of arranging.

And now, as promised, here is a specific example.

An Arrangement Deconstructed: "Once Upon a December"

There and Back Again

As a synopsis of those beginning-middle-and-end suggestions, let's examine one of my arrangements, the song "Once Upon a December" from the film *Anastasia*. My arrangement of this song has continued to attract a good deal of attention since its release in 2005. At the time of writing, it has been streamed over 70 million times. For that reason, it is a good example to discuss since it has stood the test of time.

In it, I manage to capture attention from the get-go, then follow the train of thought through till the end of the song before returning to restate the opening figure. From the opening notes in this case, we are creating an image of a magical, twirling, fantasy-like music-box dancer as the backdrop. It grabs your attention at once. It's pretty to listen to; it conveys the idea of a music-box dancer, and it lets you know what the coming story is about. Then it doesn't disappoint. It proceeds to develop the story through a sort of mini saga. The idea is to create an impressionistic effect because the whole plot of this beautifully written song is one of magic, mystery, and hope. Then when the melody comes in, the background is already there and continues the *unreality* of the wider environment as the *real* story unfolds. After a wistful episode, it takes you safely back home, so you feel complete.

Let's examine this one in detail. How did this arrangement come about? I wanted first to set the scene. I don't *always* do that, but I find that I do it naturally a lot of the time because it is like telling someone what I am going to be talking about before I actually start the conversation.

"Once upon a Time..."

The first thing I did was to establish an atmosphere for the song to subtly unfold into. To do this, I took the opening bars of the original recording and then altered the figure in such a way as to try to create the *illusion* of the music box and the magic surrounding it. I wanted to translate that magic as best I could specifically for the piano. I wasn't really trying to create the *sound* of a music box as much as the *idea* of a music box. Sometimes at the piano, I want to create the illusion of another instrument—this could be a string section, a trumpet, whatever. Well, you can't really make those *sounds* on a piano, but you can direct the listeners' attention—subtly or dramatically—to what you want them to imagine and let them fill in the blanks so that they add what they *want* to hear to what they are actually hearing.

The next step for me—and I always include this one—is to have a close look at the lyrics, to get my *head* going in the right direction along with my *heart*. I never seem to have to worry about the emotional content, but I do want to be true to the storyline presented in the lyrics; and for that reason, I like having them handy while I arrange the tune.

So now we have the music box tinkling away and the words swirling around in my head, and into that sound pool, I drip the opening melody—subtly—in such a way that the accompanying "music box" is just as important, at this point, as the actual tune.

"...There Was a Young Girl..."

The next step is to let the melody bloom so that it takes center stage. Remember, a music box is metronomic, so the rhythms and tempo stay the same throughout. It is an otherworldly, fairytale sound. That is one of the wonderful "nursery" qualities that a music box projects. So, I chose to keep that steady rhythm through the first statement of the melody. Yet on the second iteration of the melody, I stop the tinkling sound and let the melody take the limelight. Music-box tunes normally last less than a minute, and you can only do so much high-register shimmer on the piano before the ear gets tired of that sound.

"...Who Traveled to an Enchanted Land..."

Then we get to the bridge—the contrasting "B" section. Time to change the mood from the nursery to the ballroom. Now the rhythm relaxes a little, and we see the ballroom dancers twirling and swaying to the music as the character's words change from "dancing bears" (*music box*) to "someone holds me safe and warm" (*ballroom*). And as they dance, the sound grows, till on the next statement of the main theme (part "A"), we have a mix of "real" and "fantasy" as Anastasia steps more deeply into her dream. I chose to translate that mix with a chromatic line falling away from the melody because it gives the impression (to my mind) of a semidream state. In this statement of the "A" section, it felt so good that I wanted to linger in that moment a little longer, so I repeated it an extra time with slight variation. Just an artistic choice. I didn't want to leave (just as Anastasia didn't want to leave that dream).

"...and Lived There for a Time..."

Now we come to section "B" again. Anastasia is now focused on the *longing* for "someone [to hold her] safe and warm." With that yearning plea to the universe, the brilliantly constructed tune modulates up a half step, bringing an exciting reprise of the opening melody that surges upward and revels in the thrilling magic of the fantasy she is living—for a short while.

"...till at Midnight the Spell Was Broken..."

Then she realizes that it is all a dream, and she slowly comes back to her unenchanted life. The opening figure then makes a cameo appearance as the music box begins to wind down, leaving Anastasia with a magical souvenir to keep with her forever, as it dies away into dreamland whence it emerged.

That is just something I sometimes like to do—to bookend the piece. To me, it gives a feeling of completion.

So that is how I came to create that arrangement. It's exactly what I meant to say about that song. I hope this helps you to chart a course for your own musical voyage.

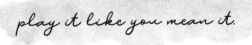

play it like you mean it.

Part Two
APPLICATION PERFORMANCE

Chapter 26

STAGE FRIGHT

Stop Staring at Me!

For most musicians, sharing their music with others is a very big reason for studying music in the first place. Many of us would like to do that but are inhibited by that all-too-common adversary, stage fright.

Boo!

Let's talk about stage fright—general comments and theory first, then practical application to help you to overcome stage fright.

One of the biggest barriers to "playing it like you mean it" is stage fright. Even just being *uncomfortable* onstage detracts from your ability to play your best. There are countless examples of very fine performers who experience that dreadful feeling of not knowing the first line of the play or the opening bars of the piece; they experience the heart palpitations and surge of adrenaline as they walk out onstage. I would like to help you conquer that awful feeling.

But let's start at the very beginning. Why do you play music anyway? Perhaps you have never sincerely answered that question. *Do you really want to perform for people in the first place?*

Some of us just want to enjoy the experience of playing the instrument for ourselves, **and that is a very fine way to be**. There is not a thing wrong with that. But it just so happens—naturally—that people who love us and are proud of us want us to share this gift. Of *course* they do, and it is out of genuine love that they make us suffer in that way! But here is the thing—YOU DON'T HAVE TO.

I'm talking here to those people who are playing piano—or other instruments—as a fulfilling hobby, and not as a profession.

It's not: *"What a shame! He has all this talent but won't play for people."* It's not "a shame." It's a ***choice***. That's all—a choice. The goal for some of you is to play piano for your personal enjoyment and not to care if anyone else ever hears you. That is a fine and worthy goal.

I may like painting and never have a desire to show my artwork to anyone. Music is like that for some people. It's a way to vent their feelings after a long day or to unlock, maybe discover, heretofore unnamed emotions because they require a nonverbal pathway to find their entry into the physical universe. The goal is to feel comfortable and *safe* at the piano, not to constantly feel the anxiety that comes from worrying that someone will ask you to perform. I am officially giving you permission to let people (gently and politely) know that "I just play for my own enjoyment." It's not a big deal.

And it's not illegal.

OK, after that—salient—detour, let's turn back to the issue at hand: **stage fright.**

Let's assume that you *want* to play in public. You're walking onstage; you say to yourself, "What's the worst thing that could happen?"

Famous last words, right?

Right.

So, let's address that, shall we?

Many people (about 50 percent according to *Psychology Today*) experience stage fright, or performance anxiety, some to an alarming degree.

Some of the world's greatest artists have suffered from stage fright.

> *"You cannot imagine what a torture the three days before a public appearance are to me. I am not fit at all for giving concerts. The crowd intimidates me, its breath suffocates me, I feel paralyzed by its curious look, and the unknown faces make me dumb."*

Guess who wrote those words.

Frédéric Chopin wrote those words to Franz Liszt.

There are numerous treatises on the subject of stage fright, some by very learned psychologists and qualified teachers, acting coaches, motivational coaches, and the like. Many offer excellent, very helpful advice on ways to combat it, such as meditation, exercises in deep breathing, practices to overcome self-doubt, dealing with social anxiety, and the like. Although these disciplines are no doubt very healthy and useful, sadly, they very often do not produce the result one hopes for, i.e., **no more stage fright.**

So, what IS stage fright? Everyone knows how it feels; it's awful! However, as far as I can tell, no one has come up with a workable definition for it—one that leads to a method for really conquering it. I believe that I can provide some genuine help with overcoming that fear of being in front of an audience. I know, I know—it's like saying I have a cure for the common cold! But I do have some ideas that I would like to share on the subject. They work for me, and I believe that if you follow these instructions, they will help you to overcome any fear you may have of being onstage.

So first of all, to be clear, stage fright is an "*unreasonable* fear of being in front of people."

So, let's state the obvious first.

If you have to speak, play, or perform in some way in front of people, *and you know you are not prepared,* then you have every reason to be nervous. That is not an *irrational* fear; that is a real, very logical fear. You aren't prepared. So, let's take that out of the discussion.

Stage Fright Redefined

For now, we are talking about an **unreasonable** fear. You have prepared yourself. You *know* the subject you are speaking about or the music you are playing. You can play it in your sleep, yet, still, you feel afraid to walk onstage. You are fearful that you will mess up. The so-called reasons for stage fright are legion. But they all have one thing in common—self-doubt, right?

Well, sort of.

I am about to tell you what I believe stage fright *actually is*—its genesis and its behavior—and, more importantly, how to overcome it.

Here is my definition:

Stage fright is nothing more nor less than having one's own attention *turned inward on oneself.*

Let me repeat that.

Stage fright is nothing more nor less than having one's own attention *turned inward on oneself.*

Read that again and again *because that truly is what stage fright consists of.*

That's all there is. There are no special cases. This is the common denominator of all stage fright experiences.

Why is that so important? Because rather than examine a million different considerations, attitudes, worries, concerns, or psychological attitudes, we go right to the generic source of the issue. We want to cut through all the nonsense, all the excellent self-worth exercises, the conquering of perceived inadequacies, and all the rest of it and get to the actual "thing" that stage fright IS!

Ismydresswrinkled?

DoIlookOK?

DidIremembertobrushmyteeth?

Ismyposturecrooked?

DoIhavespinachinmyteeth?

DoIevenknowwhatpieceIamabouttoplay?

IknewIshouldn'thavehadthatchilibeforeIwalkedonstage.

Ihavetogotothebathroom.

AmIgoingtogettothatdifficultpartandfreeze?

AmIsweating? That'sallIneed! Icouldbeplayingtennis. Myflyisunzipped. Iknewit!

Whatgivesmetherighttobehereinthefirstplace? Idon'tdeservetobeuphere!

MaybeI'lltriponthewayout.

Thebenchshouldbehigher. Thepianotunerloweareditwhenhewastuningbeforetheshow.

Thelidisontheshortstick. Itshouldbeonthelidprop!

On and on …

Rather than address each possible "reason" for an *unreasonable* fear (and the "reasons" could be infinite!), let's try to cut this psychological game off at the source. I reiterate: what do all of these conscious/subconscious considerations have in common?

They all represent one's attention being thrust inward on oneself when it should be focused outward—on the music. Just like the audience who are now listening to you play. Their attention is not on how they look; they are just listening to your beautiful music. That's what you should be doing, too, listening to the music you are creating.

Any number of things can distract your attention from the business at hand, which is to entertain your guests *(because that is what they are— your guests)*.

We will go through a series of exercises over the next few pages, but here is a precept to consider: **you must have the viewpoint *(and it is only a viewpoint)* that you don't *want* or *need* anything from your audience; rather, you are there to *give* them something.** That is the first step in conquering stage fright.

Let me give you a real-life example.

The kind of attitude you need to have as you walk onstage is the same as that of, say, a tech person who works with the theater. Watch him or her walk onstage before the show and adjust the drum kit, the cables, or the music stands. He knows he is not performing; he is just doing a job, so he does it. If the mic stand is the wrong height and won't cooperate, he just keeps working with it till it's right. You can't start the show till he's done!

If you suddenly told him "You know, everyone is watching every move you make," *(which they **are**)* he still wouldn't care because he is entirely focused on the job at hand. It just happens that he does his routine job in front of a thousand people. He's used to it.

Why is he so at ease? Because he honestly doesn't *want* anything from the audience, *including approval*. He's not asking for applause, although he occasionally gets some. He is making the stage ready for a great performance. He is doing something for *you*, the audience. And that is the key. You are there to *give* something to the audience, and if they like your gift, they will probably say thank-you by way of applause.

Here is a true-life story of how I came to learn about the attention principle. This actually happened to me many years ago. It was early in my concert career, and I was a little bit nervous. It was the first performance of that particular show, and I was going over the program rapidly in my head. I was a little concerned about a particular passage in a Chopin ballade that I was playing in the concert.

I was well prepared but still a bit anxious. It was about 15 minutes before show time. I was standing backstage preparing myself mentally to go on. As I was waiting, a close friend came to the dressing room to wish me luck. She had her five-year-old boy with her. It happened to be his birthday, and he had just got some toy or other that he loved. Well, he started in at once telling me all about his party, his friends, and his toys, and I was charmed by this little narrative. *I became genuinely interested in him and his story.* For those few minutes, as I listened with rapt attention to a little boy talk about his remarkable adventures, I never noticed the time passing! Suddenly it was time to go on! I was a little stunned, to be honest. I quickly gathered my thoughts to put myself back into performance mode, and I played the show without incident. However, I made myself a rule not to entertain guests within an hour of the show.

Yet the next day, as I was debriefing myself regarding the show, I realized that my attention had been moved—rather abruptly—away from my own musings and onto this cherub's story. Children do that. They are all about themselves, and when they are telling a story, you are both interested and enchanted. Ergo, your attention is drawn at once away from yourself and onto this child, who believes the world revolves around himself—as do all little children. **I realized, in retrospect, that during that entire time I had suffered no feelings of anxiety**.

Although I didn't have time to analyze it then, I had stumbled upon the mechanism of *attention control*, and it was then—about 35 years ago—that I subconsciously formulated this postulate that I am sharing with you now. "Out of the mouths of babes …"

From that point on, I explored it, tried it out, and found that if I could control the direction of my attention, I could conquer performance anxiety. It did me a great deal of good.

Here is another example. Did you ever have a person at work, or even a casual acquaintance, look at you and say, "Do you feel OK?" "Are you sure you're all right?" "Is that the dress you're wearing to the party?" Or even a friend, in fun, say, "Did you choose that shirt on purpose, or did you lose a bet? Hah, hah!" You think "Why'd he make that joke? Do I look funny? Is there something wrong with my outfit?"

Whether friendly or not, the result is the same: **your attention is *thrust* rather suddenly inward upon yourself!** And speaking of "friendly *or not*," turning one's attention on oneself is an age-old trick of intimidation: at a job interview, a sporting event, or a competition of any kind. That's why coaches never *ever* let their athletes or performers mingle with other contestants before an event.

A stellar example of this device (and it *is* a device) is that of a witness being cross-examined by an aggressive prosecuting attorney. The witness, if honest, is not worried about his truth; he is worried that he will be coerced into saying something that he didn't mean to say. Sometimes the strength of a hostile prosecutor lies largely in his ability to turn a witness against himself. It's not about truth or facts; it's about getting a person to cross-examine himself.

"So, let me see, you *say* your name is Fred, but you don't actually *remember* hearing the priest say your name at the christening, do you?"

"Well, no, I don't remember! I was very young at the time...I just always assumed..."

"You *assumed*?"

"Well, if you put it *that* way, I guess I am not *positive* that my name is Fred..."

"So, you just took your parents' word for it?

"I, uh...I guess so."

"I rest my case."

And so on, down the rosy path of self-doubt.

OK, so now what do you do so as not to fall prey to your innermost fear? *"You have been weighed on the scales and found wanting."*

What **do** you do?

What you do is you turn your attention *outward*; which is to say, don't join the jury against you. That's two against one! **Refuse to self-criticize.** *That happens in the practice room.* Once you are onstage, the piece is how it is. You prepared the best you can. If you want to improve it, do it at your next practice session. Don't do that onstage.

Just to let you know that I practice what I preach, here is a real-life example of how I handled it a few years ago when I experienced a musical train wreck in one of my performances in front of 600 people. One of the pieces on the program was the *Fantaisie-Impromptu* by Chopin. Well, I had some sort of mental block and crashed in the first eight bars. I stopped, started again, and crashed again. What did I do? I got up from the piano and said to the audience, with a sort of mischievous smile, **"I guess I don't know it! But you should hear it someday; it is really beautiful!"** (I really did exactly that.)

And then I introduced the next piece. And the rest of the concert went on without incident. Did I refuse to turn my attention inward? Not really. I didn't have to. You see, I am so comfortable with the premise that it doesn't even *occur* to me to look inward when onstage. As I have said, I can laugh at myself (thank goodness!). I have made a fool of myself onstage (numerous times, I am sorry to say), but I don't get into self-chiding while I am performing. I went on to the next piece and finished the concert. And the next day I took the piece out of the program till I would have time—*in the practice room*—to really learn it, find out what happened, and not let it happen again. **But it didn't ruin the rest of the concert.**

It could easily have been a *Terrible! Horrible! No Good! Very Bad!* experience. But it wasn't. I really didn't even feel that bad about it. Why should I? It happened; I carried on and enjoyed the rest of the show.

This really happened. However, I do not recommend it! I recommend practicing enough so that that can never happen!

If, at the after-party, someone had said, "You sure had a train wreck in the Chopin!"

I would *(honestly!)* have said, "I KNOW!! Is that crazy or what? Pass me the chocolate chip cookies." (In reality, they all had the good taste not to mention it, but I'm sure they all *remembered* it.) An ancillary reward for having this attitude is that it puts your audience more at ease too. "If *he* doesn't think it's a big deal, I guess it isn't. Maybe he did it on purpose."

You see, I have made it such a habit to control where my attention goes that I am not in danger of making such an error. I just don't. It gets put "on hold" till I am back in the practice room. Therefore, the person who *refuses* to have his attention manipulated *(by himself or others)* will always come out feeling OK. It does not mean she will win the case, get the job, or not miss any notes. It means that she is her own boss, that no one but herself is in charge of how she feels and, by extension, how she speaks or performs.

Now, can we fix this inclination to self-examine, to self-chastise, blah-blah-blah?

Yes.

Is this an *easy* fix?

No! Definitely not!

But is it possible?

Definitely yes!

It is a **simple**, **universal** fix.

It can also apply globally to your personal travails in self-confidence in any public forum. It works for anyone because it is a quasi "law" of psychology.

*Side note: I am not a psychologist and do not pretend to be. I am an empiricist. I **made up** this quasi "law." But it works.*

And Now, Ladies and Gentlemen, for the Solution!

Following are exercises to help you form the habit of putting your attention *outward*, where it *belongs* in these instances.

The whole thrust of these exercises will be to learn to take control of your attention so that *you* decide where your attention goes. Hours, days, or weeks can pass between steps; that is not important. What is important is to give these exercises an honest try. Really *do* what they suggest, with understanding, and I promise you that you will begin to lose your fear of being in front of people.

Exercise One (at the piano)

If at all possible, do this with a grand piano. Perhaps there is one at your teacher's house, the music school, or a church.

All by yourself, when no one else is around, walk around the piano, look at the hammers, and touch the strings, the whole case; "get" how good it feels as an object. Study it more carefully than you ever have before—the individual parts, how beautiful it is as a whole, and what a glorious invention it is! How could someone have built such an astonishing machine out of wood, iron, leather, felt, nuts and bolts, and springs and wires—10,000 moving parts? Literally! Look into the harp, study the hammers and dampers as you play some notes, watch what happens, and really search into the workings of it. Crawl underneath, lie on the floor for a bit, and be astonished at the massive timbers that support this colossal beast. Don't let it have any secrets. *Look, look, look!* Study! Do this until you discover something new about the physical characteristics, its quirks and idiosyncrasies, if you will, or something unexpected and peculiar that had somehow escaped your notice before.

Do this as long as you like, and as many times as you like over time, but do it thoroughly and sincerely. From it, learn something you never knew about the nuances of making a sound come out of the piano. Do you want it to do what you ask of it? Then understand it!

Notice, now, where your attention is. It's on the instrument, not on you.

Exercise Two

By yourself. Sit at the piano, think of a piece of music that you know, and start to play it (with no sheet music). Now, purposely make a lot of mistakes. Just play any old thing. If you are not used to improvising, now is a good time to try. Play something horrible, awful—something the world has never heard (and shouldn't!). Never mind what. Notice that nothing *bad* happens—except maybe a little cacophony.

After you have banged out any old notes for a while, next play something beautiful, divine, touching, and wonderful. Just a single-note phrase will do or a familiar tune that you love, a song or a classical melody that you know well. Think about what you are playing and nothing else. Listen to the notes. *Feel* the keys as you press them, now soft, now loud. Experience the true "*art* of playing the piano."

See if you can play these notes without judgment from either yourself or that which you perceive from others. How? By just listening to what you are playing and being *genuinely interested* in how each note follows the preceding one, how a melody in its fledgling state is nothing but a sequence of individual notes, each succeeding one upon the other until a pattern emerges and a new melody is born. No one is listening, and it doesn't matter what you play. If you don't know what to play, just play a scale, but play it elegantly, beautifully. *Care* about that scale!

Do this until you can do it without judging the quality of the music you come up with, remembering that this is an exercise in *listening without judgment*. If you do find yourself saying "That was awful," remember what this drill is for—listening without criticism. Smile at yourself and continue the exercise. Do this until you are doing nothing but sitting at the piano, *listening* to the sounds you are making, feeling comfortable right where you are, and experiencing the joy of touching the keys and having them respond. **Study that experience.** Do this exercise for a long time and repeatedly. It is what your playing is all about: *listening*. You have moved any inward attention you may have had going on outward. *You have done this without any effort on your part.* You are not *forcing* your attention to go outward; you are simply enjoying what's going on outside your brain. *You are genuinely interested.* And that is the key.

Notice where your attention is—on the notes you are playing, not on yourself.

Exercise Three

Sit at the piano and *imagine* you are sitting in front of an audience member who is a friend who loves the way you play. Play something that you know really well and that you genuinely **love**. In your mind, tell this person all about this piece of music, how wonderful it is and how you hope they like it the way that you like it. As a matter of fact, speak out loud even though you are the only one there. Talk about it sincerely. Don't make anything up; just speak from the heart about this piece of music and visualize your friend listening intently, maybe adding comments, enjoying how much YOU love the music. Do this until you have really got the feeling that you have told this friend everything you can about that piece of music.

Notice where your attention is: it's on the music and on your friend.

Exercise Four

This one is best done **with a close friend, family member, or anyone with whom you feel entirely SAFE.** Someone with whom you can be yourself, without fear of criticism. Tell them beforehand what you are doing. Sit across a table from them or in comfortable chairs (but not at the piano), just **be there,** and talk with your friend. Don't try to be interesting. Just chat; don't necessarily discuss anything in particular, just enjoy being with your friend. You might be boring or bored but don't worry about it. This is not about entertainment. Notice how comfortable it is to *not have to be interesting,* just enjoying the other's company. Do this for however long it takes till you are genuinely at ease, maybe laughing at how silly it feels or getting bored with the exercise, talking about anything you want to, including that this is a silly exercise about stage fright. Each time your attention goes inward on yourself (How do I look? Do I sound foolish? I don't have anything interesting to say, and so on), *do nothing about it.* Don't even try to "fix" it. **Just notice.** Do this until you realize (in retrospect) that you have hardly been thinking about yourself at all; rather, you are sharing a delightful experience with someone you love. That is what playing for someone is all about. It is a shared experience between you and them.

Notice where your attention is.
It's on your friend or on this silly exercise.

Exercise Five

Have that same friend look at you while you sit there quietly. She can compliment how you look, but you must sit still. Have her stare at you, walk around you, look at your ear, look at your nose, look closely at what you are wearing, and examine and talk about everything about you until it is "flat." Nothing she can do will make you start to self-examine. No apologies. As a matter of fact, you are amused by **watching her watch *you***. This is a fun game. **Notice her noticing you.**

She is *gently* trying to turn your attention inward, and you—***you!***—emboldened now because you know the rules of the game, smile or laugh as you refuse to turn your attention inward. You say to yourself, "This is how I look." Period. If you need a little nudge to *not* look inward, just look around the room. Admire the furniture, notice what she is wearing, silently compliment her on her taste in clothes. Just keep this up until you have an "aha!" moment or get bored with it.

Notice where your attention is. It is on the game, not on your nose!

Exercise Six

Now do the same with two or more friends. Talk about *all those thoughts that go through your head when someone looks at you*. Talk about them. Talk about being afraid of making mistakes, being nervous, sweating, or whatever because you trust these people who love you, and they are not going to make fun of you.

Get it out in the open: "I think people think my posture is poor, my feet are too big, and my nose is crooked." Maybe your nose *is* crooked! Talk way too much about your imperfections until it gets boring or silly.

Guess what! We ALL have imperfections (*except maybe Julia Roberts!*).

Notice that even though, in this exercise, your attention is gently turned in on yourself, nothing horrible has happened. *You are learning to laugh at yourself.* When you can honestly do that, you are well on your way to conquering stage fright because no matter how diligently you work at this there will be times that your attention is thrust inward. And at those times, you *must* learn to laugh at yourself! (I got a birthday card once that said it beautifully: *"If you can't laugh at yourself, look in the mirror and see what everyone else is laughing at."* I love it!)

Notice that even with your attention turned inward—on purpose—nothing bad happened. **It became what it truly is: a GAME.**

When you have genuinely found out that being amused about some of your perceived flaws or imperfections wasn't so bad, go on to the next exercise.

Exercise Seven

Sit at the piano. Ask some friends or family to sit in the piano room and just talk with you. In this exercise, they don't say anything necessarily *about* you; they just talk with you as you sit at the piano. Are you nervous just sitting at the piano, even though you are not playing anything? **Notice that.** Just be there and have a chat with them. How do they like the room you are in? Did they know that you got this piano seven years ago? Do they have a piano? You always wanted one, and now you have it. Show them your piano. Look at some of the details of it now that you know all the intricacies (from completing Exercise One). Have they any idea what happens when you press a key—that it initiates a host of sophisticated events that converge to culminate in a sound? Did they ever really think about the fact that to make a sound on the piano, the lever has to set off a whole series of Rube Goldberg-like sequences before it hits the string? Show them the hammer hitting the string. Take them on a tour of the instrument—the massive great legs holding up this elegant monster, the beautiful finish, the weight alone! Tell them some interesting facts. For example, an upright weighs 400–500 pounds, and a concert grand can weigh over 1,000! Half a ton! (True!) Aren't those fascinating facts for the next trivia game?

Notice where your attention is: on the piano and your friends, not on you.

Exercise Eight

Now it is time to play for someone. Choose a piece that you can play really well, even if it is just a portion of a piece of music. Ask a family member or friend (another musician if possible) to listen to you play but—and this is truly important—listen *with* them **as though you are both listening to someone *else* play the song**. These are people who want to help you overcome your nervousness about performing for people. They are on your side. Talk, interrupt your own playing, or actually stop in the middle, if you feel like it, to tell them about what you just played. Tell them about the origin of the song, what the words mean, or why you like it. Tell them all about what you are playing. Tell them what key it's in, where it lies on the keyboard, and how it falls beautifully under the fingers. Tell them why you learned it in the first place. Admire the music; draw their attention to all those ever-so-subtle intricacies of harmony, voicing, phrasing, and dynamics that you love to put into the music when you play it. Examine it closely—**out loud**. Does it feel good under the hand? Do they think people in general like this piece? Discuss the music, the music, *the music!* As you are talking and visiting, move the bench, adjust the lid up or down, readjust the music rack so it is just where you like it, turn pages of the sheet music, and *take your time with all of it*. **Get comfortable doing these things in front of people.**

Do this till you feel relaxed and comfortable playing with the instrument, talking in and out of your piano playing. After you have done this for a while, just shut up and play the whole thing for your friends. Later on, when you are comfortable playing for one or two people, you will realize

Play It Like You Mean It

that an audience is just a whole bunch of friends you haven't met yet—a whole bunch of "one or two people."

Notice where your attention is. By now you should be on your way to *wanting* to share something with your listeners. You are anxious to show them this piece of music. You are starting to realize that *you are truly giving them a gift.*

Exercise Nine

So, let's move on to the next logical step. This one is really a mental exercise wherein you start to experience a paradigm shift.

You will be playing a piece that you really know well in front of a small, friendly audience. This should preferably be some of the other piano students in your teacher's class. Or it could be a group of friends that you invite over, telling them that you are practicing getting over stage fright. Just admit it. It's like AA. "My name is John, and I suffer from stage fright." Just enough people to feel like an actual audience—a situation in which you might normally feel anxiety, or just nervousness. But remember—*you are on a journey*, a path toward *freedom*, the freedom that abounds in sharing a part of yourself with others through the wonderful world of musical sounds. Start to feel *privileged* instead of *anxious*. Because you *are* privileged! How many people get to do what you are doing right this minute? **Decide to change your own mind.**

Start to *like* your audience and see them as *friends*. Because that's what they are. Otherwise, they wouldn't be there.

The point of this exercise is to create a paradigm shift in which you re-categorize the audience from "strangers" to "friends I have not yet met." They *will* be your friends after the performance because, through the magic that is inherent in music—if you play it sincerely—you can connect with people you have never met in a very personal way. I promise. Enjoy that connection. Music is a great icebreaker, a great entry point into a conver-

164

sation, or a way to make new friends. Be friendly and invite your audience to be friendly. *Want* them to have a good time. And they will be much less critical of your playing than you are. That I can pretty much guarantee.

Notice that you are *causatively* moving your attention onto the piano, the listeners, the room, and the music you are about to play. Do this on purpose until it becomes the most natural thing in the world. Because that is where your attention should be when you are playing: on entertaining your friends.

Exercise Ten

Now it is time to play some music for an actual audience. This will probably be the recital piece(s) that you have been working on. The goal here is to get you to *look forward* to playing for people. You are going to play a recital piece, and here is your frame of mind: *"I have worked on this piece; I know it really well. I really like it, and I think they will too. I have this gift of sound all wrapped up in a package (the piece) that I am giving them. My playing of it is their opening the package. I can't wait till they see what's inside! I chose it myself (or my teacher did), and it is nothing more nor less than a **gift** to these friendly people. They **want** to like it. They **want** me to show it to them. I will actually **enjoy** playing in front of people."*

Summary

OK, we are done with these exercises. Now let's just talk about playing for people. Do it as often as you can, for anyone, at any time. ***Casually!*** Just sit down and show someone part of the piece you're working on. It's not a "performance"; it's not a test; it is more of a discussion, albeit a musical one. Go ahead; make mistakes. Who cares? BIG DEAL! Don't listen to the mistakes. Just get the whole "WAH" of it as you play. "Ain' no big thing!"

Honestly, take a look at **what you are like when you are not performing.** Look at your attitude when you are showing a friend the chess set that you just bought because you always wanted to play chess but never learned; you are genuinely intrigued by the game, and you are discovering the intricacies of how the pieces move, how *fascinating* that is. And notice how your attention is all about the game, the board, the rook, the pawn, and the knight, and not about you.

You are no longer overcoming fear; you are experiencing the JOY of sharing your voice with others. Your mental attitude has moved from one of *fear* to one of *joy*. You have conquered most of your fears. And by continuing to refer back to these little exercises as you need to, you will change your own *philosophy* of how you play and why you play.

This is the JOY of playing for people. It's about how much playing the piano means to you, what an emotional release it is, and how much fun you have when you are all by yourself and can let your heart and mind wander. And you discover yet another wonderful ingredient in the music that you have played for ages but had somehow escaped your notice.

Caveat Re: Judgment

There will *always* be listeners who make silent judgments about the way you play. Always. Everyone does it, just as everyone makes silent judgments about how every other person drives his car. We just do it. It's not a mean or malicious thing (most of the time). It's a *human* characteristic, and it helps us to grow, to learn from our own and others' mistakes, and to evolve. I am sure that *you* do that when you hear others play: "I would have played that phrase differently." That is the most natural thing in the world to do. Everyone has an opinion. This is why you must embrace the fact that judgment is going to be there. And notice that nothing bad happened. An opinion just came and went.

Innocuous judgment happens all the time. Try driving down the street and looking at your surroundings. Try *not* to have an opinion about what you see. What do you think of that building? Ugly? Pretty?

"That's a gorgeous tree!"

"Why would they put a traffic circle right *THERE?*"

It's just part of life. You do it; I do it. You like something; you don't like something. It's hard to look at anything without—at least subconsciously—making some sort of judgment, whether aesthetic, logical, or even amusing. It happens. So, bearing that in mind, don't focus on it. Just focus on the music.

However, if at any time while you are onstage, you find your attention wandering inward, just look out at the room, start counting the ceiling tiles, windows, rows of seats, or faces, and just notice anything that will direct your attention outside of yourself!

(And while you're at it, look for where the exit signs are in case all this fails and you have to make a speedy escape! Oops! Did I say that out loud? Freudian slip! I meant to say "Good luck!")*

Chapter 27

PROGRAMMING

How to Get from Hither to Yon without Going Hither and Thither!

Let's say that you have a performance coming up, and you are not sure what to play. It could be a recital, wedding, memorial service, a party, a corporate event, a holiday celebration, or—my favorite—a concert in a performing arts center. No matter what the occasion is, you need to decide what to play and in what order. How do you prepare a "good" program? It is not about me or what I can do; it is about their enjoyment. What do I believe they would like to **experience?**

Classical programs are traditionally put together in an orderly fashion, either chronologically, from earliest composers to the most recent, or by featuring works of only one or two composers. Or it could be organized by musical period: Classical, Romantic, Baroque, or Impressionistic, in any order, with some short pieces in between sometimes. Because pieces from the classical repertoire tend to be so much longer than those in the pop field, there are fewer individual pieces played, and the order in which they are programmed is often done from a scholarly perspective for a learned audience. Many classical audience members, myself included, are looking for intellectual stimulation in addition to the hearing of fine music, and we hope to learn something about the composer and the pieces being played. That is why classical recitals are considered by some listeners as "stuffy" when in fact, to those of us who love classical music, those performances are invigorating, exciting, and intellectually energizing.

In a pop concert, on the other hand, you have a great deal more freedom. Same with playing for a specialized event. It's mostly up to you. It's all about taking the listener on a "night out" on a journey of your choosing, without *logic* necessarily being a part of the journey or the destination. The one criterion that I use is "is it entertaining?" By "entertaining," I do not mean lighthearted, insubstantial filler. I mean have you given them something of genuine artistic value for the entire time you are onstage and is it worth their time to listen to you?

I write programs all the time. Following here is a brief outline of how I approach creating an interesting one. This is just a guide and, of course, my opinion. There is no "right" way to structure a performance, and it can be as long or short as the occasion dictates. Because there are so many variables, I would just like to boil it down to some general guidelines, assuming that you have control over what you will play. I plan it out based on the following considerations.

Say you are hosting a party with friends. Even if this is in a concert setting, think of all the tunes you play. Which ones usually bring an emotional response from the listeners? People will not necessarily remember what titles you played, but they will remember how they *felt* when you played them. Remember that you are giving them something real and intimate and that you want it to be something they *want*. Sometimes performers make the mistake of doing their "best" stuff, whether or not the audience wants to hear it.

Decide on the length of the program. For a recital or concert, the normal length is 45 minutes to an hour. In a performing arts center, this usually consists of two halves with a 15-minute intermission. Each half is 45 minutes to an hour long.

Here are some tips:

Step one. Start programming from the end.

What is the LAST thing you want the people to hear as they are leaving? Depending on your style, persona, and the type of performances you do, ask yourself the following questions:

Do you want a showy grand finale?

Do you want the audience talking excitedly as they leave?

Do you want to ease out of the last piece and leave the audience in a reflective mood?

Is your last piece a long medley that is a little bit of everything that encapsulates the program?

Put a good deal of thought into how you want the visitors to *feel* about the evening's entertainment as they leave, for that is the thing they will talk about with their friends as they exit the hall. They want to feel satisfied, complete, and involved in the ending of your show and feel that they got their money's worth. One of my most successful closers is a medley of songs from *Phantom of the Opera*. I almost always close my show with that medley because I play it well, my audiences love those songs, and the arrangements are emotionally powerful. I want them to walk away having had an experience that they cherish.

Step two. Decide on the beginning.

The opening of the show is just as important—first impressions and all that.

What is the nature and character of your performance?

What is the very *first* thing you want them to hear?

Will you start by speaking to the audience?

Or with an exciting piece of music?

Or with a contemplative song that sets the mood for a warm, cozy evening?

Think about your *signature style* and start out strong with that. I have experimented with several different openings, and I can't really tell you that one was "better" than another. However, in each case I worked very hard to make the opening strong, attention-grabbing, and very much **me.**

For example, I have started by walking onto the stage in the dark, sitting down at the piano, and without saying a word, just starting to play a piece (in this case, "Malagueña" by Ernesto Lecuona) that starts out quietly and builds throughout. As I play, the lights come up—very slowly—till the stage is dramatically lit and the piece grows, seven minutes later, to its exciting conclusion, ending on a brightly lit stage. After the bow and applause, I say my first words of welcome to the audience.

Another variation is to begin in the dark with one of the pieces that is relatively quiet, something that is easy for you to play, maybe a beautiful ballad that is not technically demanding. An example of that, for me, is "Somewhere in Time," from the movie by that name. Fairly easy to play but gorgeous and moving. That way you have a chance to warm up your fingers in front of a live audience, since you don't usually get to warm up before you walk onstage.

A completely different opening, and one that I do the most often, is to simply walk out onstage, acknowledge the applause, welcome the audience, and segue into a monologue introducing the first piece. I want to put them at ease, so I start with a bit of lighthearted humor because that is "me."

Whatever you do, you need to be sincere about it. Every performer has different personality traits, and you can use some of the results of the exercises in earlier chapters about finding out which of your characteristics as a person best suit you onstage. What do people think of who you are? Are you sophisticated? Rural? Formal? Casual? Funny? Serious? Just create a larger-than-life version (or caricature) of who you really are.

As for what your opening words (and the rest of your monologues) should be, I am an advocate of writing exact scripts because that's what works best for me, but that's an entirely personal choice. My scripts are not just made-up things to say for the sake of it; they say something about me and my real personality. That is why they come across as sincere. Because they *are*. A dear friend of mine who is also a brilliant comic has the ability to improvise what he has to say and sound wonderful doing it. He has a few subjects that knows he is going to cover beforehand, but that is about it. I, however, am much more comfortable adhering exactly to a script. He and I have worked together on hundreds of shows. Each of us uses his own style, and it works perfectly. You just need to be who you are and not try to pretend to be something else.

Step three. The body of the program

General advice: keep it interesting. I like a program to ebb and flow, with tempo or key changes. For example, try not to play two songs back-to-back in a medley *in the same key*. People subconsciously get tired of hearing songs in the same key. Always remembering that it is about the **audience**; you want them to be *moved*, to experience emotions—not just hear a favorite song. So, choose songs that contain intense emotion (in your rendition). Happy, exciting, sad, nostalgic, just a *lot* of it, whatever that feeling is. In other words, you don't want "filler" or "downtime."

A word on silences between songs—when the applause for one song is over, start your spoken introduction right away. Or if you are getting a sip of water, for example, have a little something to say before and after. Silence onstage is deadly. It seems about five times as long as in real life.

You want every moment of the performance to be worthwhile. That is always a judgment call, but do try to avoid playing a song just because you can't think of something better to play. Certainly, not every song will please every audience member, but pleasing every audience member must at least be your goal.

Summary

In a nutshell, *think it through*. I spend several days—weeks sometimes—writing, rewriting, moving songs around from one half of the program to the other and thinking of new threads to connect one song to the next. Sometimes my scripts determine which song to play next. As I mentioned earlier, when working out the route an evening takes, it does not necessarily have to be a logical progression. In other words, you may find that after you have played an emotion-packed ballad and the audience is still sighing, they may need a break. You are in charge of the flow of the evening. Sometimes you can change gears utterly and follow a tear-jerker with a novelty tune (use your judgment!). Just let the audience "have" the afterglow of the song *before* you change the subject to a light, easygoing piece. It's like serving a lemon sorbet between the fish and the main course at a fine dinner. The emotionally lean, smile-inducing offering is a palate cleanser and, after a heavy dose of heartstring tugging, can often afford a "safe haven," giving the crowd the time they need to recover from the substantial musical entrée they have just enjoyed. As always,

play it like you mean it!

Chapter 28

SHOWING OFF!

Look, Ma! No Hands! Or *Three* Hands!

Somewhere along the way, you will probably want to learn a novelty piece, or a "stunt," something that is a crowd-pleaser, just for laughs, or to show off. I would listen to pianists who play stride, pianists who work at places like Disney World, for example. Honky-tonk or ragtime, maybe some pieces that were written for piano roll in the early 1900s.

There are books and books of delightful little tunes that are just right for a certain slot in a certain situation. You don't need several—maybe one or two.

A good example for piano is "Dizzy Fingers" by Zez Confrey written in 1923. It is fast and makes people smile but is not that difficult. It just sounds like it is. But your choice *does* need to be something impressive—not necessarily "hard" to play, just delightful. You choose one that makes people smile and say, "Oh please play that … 'Bumble Boogie.' " That famous adaptation by Jack Fina of the classical Rimsky-Korsakov orchestral work "Flight of the Bumblebee," for example, is not difficult but gets a great response. It makes everyone happy.

Learn your show-off piece well—no mistakes—and do it with a lighthearted attitude, maybe some funny, overdone hand or arm movements; maybe make a little joke about it. But you do it your way. Just be sure that they know you don't take yourself seriously. It's just for fun.

My favorite "stunt" is an arrangement that I made of the song "A Dream is a Wish Your Heart Makes" from Disney's *Cinderella*. It is not lighthearted or silly, but I put it in the category of a "show piece" because I made an arrangement of it **for the left hand alone**. It's quite pretty, actually, and impressive (and it's difficult to play). People enjoy watching it. It looks and sounds impossible. And after all, don't we all love watching a juggler do something seemingly impossible? I sure do. I introduce it with a lot of silliness and take a big "ta-da!" bow at the end.

But that is *not* something I would play at a club or a party; it's for the concert stage. So along the way, while preparing your recital pieces, take the time to learn (in addition to what your teacher prescribes) a novelty piece that has stood the test of time, one that you can enjoy playing in any setting. You can play it for the next 50 years because those sorts of pieces, by their very nature, never go out of style.

Chapter 29

SCRIPT WRITING

You Are Onstage Now; *Say* Something!

You need to speak in such a way that people can both hear and understand what you have to say. In a recital hall, you will not usually have a microphone, so you need to be able to project without sounding affected. How to do that? Take some lessons. If you are attending college, go over to the drama department and take acting as an elective. If you are an adult who is already playing professionally, listen to yourself on tape and see if you need to participate in something like Toastmasters International.

You need to make people feel at ease, so they are not desperately trying to understand what you just said. If you feel that you are bad at speaking publicly, you can keep it short, but you still have to say something! Like anything else, public speaking is a skill. And any skill can be learned or improved upon. Like it or not, you are in the entertainment business, and public speaking is part of that.

If you are funny, use a funny monologue—well rehearsed so that you don't stumble. If you are a serious person, say something educational or fascinating. But, again, polish your script, so you don't sound either artificial or unsure of what comes next. Learn these techniques from your coach. And do what he or she says. The main point is *talk to the audience*. Make friends with them at the beginning, and they will remain your friends throughout the evening. Some people are great speaking extempore, off-the-cuff. Me? I am most "spontaneous" when I am well rehearsed.

In public speaking, the goal is for the speech to sound natural *but probably a little slower than you would normally speak* and louder and more precise than the normal, understandable level and tempo of talking to another person in daily life.

Pay close attention to any host or emcee on shows like American Idol or news anchors, game show hosts, and so on. If you start to really listen to and emulate the speakers you admire, it will be of great value to you. You can even speak along with them and get a feel for the tempo of their speech. Hint: you will notice that many of them move their lips more than you might consider "normal." That is a very helpful technique that you, too, can use when practicing to keep from mumbling and to make yourself understood. Practice privately, really *over-moving* your lips when you enunciate. A remarkable example of that, that I have noticed (and it is just my observation) is the way that Emma Watson moves her lips when she speaks. She is the actress who played Hermione in the *Harry Potter* movies. Watch her on YouTube.

Like many aspects of performing, speaking sometimes needs to be overdone, bigger than life—at least at first. Then you practice, practice, practice and temper it so you don't sound like a robot. Once again, this practice is to get you to *change a frame of mind*. You must just approach the act of speaking from a different viewpoint so that you can speak more clearly onstage than you used to. The whole point, after all, is to be understood and to maintain a natural sound to your voice.

As for actually writing things to say, it should be fun and rewarding to find out that you *can* write a script. My style is to make fun of myself, and I present myself as a little absentminded onstage, a sort of pseudo-professor type, always family-friendly, and I laugh at myself. It's a stage persona that I have chosen over the years *based on real characteristics of mine*; then I emphasize them—a caricature of the real me. I am also, by nature, very silly, so that is part of the mockup. I suggest you do the same. Examine yourself carefully. Ask friends what attributes they would most use to describe you to someone who doesn't know you. Or just notice how people behave toward you or how a friend would impersonate you. Are you very introspective, serious, and pensive, or are you outgoing, electric, and over-the-top when you tell a story? Do you love relating interesting facts about your own history? Do you have a favorite hobby that you love talking about? Are you a wordsmith? Do you love to engage people in conversation, or would you rather be up in front of the classroom giving a lecture? Do you move your hands and arms a lot when you speak?

Find your personal style more precisely by getting outside yourself and *observing yourself* at parties and gatherings when you feel you are your funniest or most engaging, your most charming or touching, or…or… Later at home, make a note of what you said, what you did, and who you were "being."

I learned that and a lot more from my mom. When we were growing up, mom loved having parties at our (modest) home. She was a wonderful host, and the gatherings were always lively, casual, and fun, with lots of music. At the end of the evening, as we four siblings were all cleaning up, she would take us into the kitchen and let us know what we had or hadn't done to be excellent hosts. Were we good conversationalists? Did we make sure no one was standing alone without someone to talk to? Did we make sure glasses were refilled and serving plates easily available? Did each of us speak to every person at the party? In short, *did we focus our attention on our guests* to make sure they *all* had a good time? We learned from an early age that the party was not about **us**. To this day, when I am a guest at a party, I remember those "rules," and I act as a sort of "assistant host." I can't help it.

That is a very good lesson to learn, and it applies equally to your work on the stage. You need to be the host and talk to everyone in the audience; you need to make friends with them, appreciate the fact that they chose to come to your party, and really—sincerely—*want* them to have a great time.

That training has also helped me, years later, to write my scripts. Here are some tips.

Always have a pencil and paper, (or a phone recorder) at the ready to write down funny or fascinating snippets of conversation, no matter who said them. Develop a radar for funny events or weird juxtapositions of places or products. Simply wrong or illogical signs you may see on a building or billboard can be the seeds of an amusing idea you may have three years later. Even if you are good at extemporaneous speaking, I still recommend preparing an outline of what you are going to say so that you don't leave out an important or germane topic.

If you are speaking to your audience from an instructor's viewpoint, do all your research on the subject, learn some interesting facts, and then close the computer and see what you have come away with. Don't just paraphrase Wikipedia. Everyone has access to facts these days. Instead start talking (to yourself) about how the music has affected you. Supposing you are performing a piece by J. S. Bach for a classical audience. Don't just tell them things they all learned in school. Think outside the "Bachs"! For example, how do you suppose Bach remembered the names of his 20 children? How did they work out using the bathroom? The harpsichord? More importantly, how did his two wives manage? When did he even have time to write a bazillion pieces of music? He must have *had* to write all that music to feed his family. Did he really get into a sword fight (yes, he did) with another musician (one of his students) in a public place? (Yes, he did.) What does all this tell you about his character? Talk about it. Have a discussion with one of your musically educated friends and talk about how the piece you are going to be playing came to be. Did he write it during dinner? After the kids were in bed? What frame of mind was the composer in when he wrote it? Just find really interesting tidbits and share them through your own looking glass. Concentrate not so much on historical facts as personality, daily chores, and the art and cultural environment in which Bach lived. Try to walk in the composer's shoes. Read a good biography. Where did they get their groceries? Talk about them the way you talk to your friends about how you spend your *own* time away from the piano.

Side note: I love listening to Miles Hoffman and Fred Child on National Public Radio music stations. They always come up with some interesting little-known fact or a new take on the piece that is about to be played. They are two great examples of what we are talking about. Of course, they are both the best in the business, so really study how they do what they do.

If you are just starting out, create a short statement about the piece that you are about to play, in your own style. Maybe you want to draw your audience's attention to a particular section of the piece or the flow of the entire work. "Listen to how Rachmaninoff starts out creating a feeling of doom and then builds and builds to a shattering climax before it turns all the way around and makes its descent back into the darkness whence it emerged." Get creative and throw out what doesn't work or that sounds stilted. Most of all, if you are nervous about doing this, find what *genuinely, sincerely* excites you about the music you are about to play and tell them *why* it excites you or consults your intellect or how it makes you feel. Be honest. Talk to the audience the way you talk to one friend.

If you choose the humorous route:

Make 'Em Laugh! Don't Be Afraid of *Stoopid* Ideas!

You don't have to be a Steve Martin or a Kevin Hart. You wouldn't usually expect a belly laugh—well, I guess you might. But ordinarily you want a smile, a giggle, a feel-good laugh. If you are already a very funny person onstage, then you probably don't need to be reading this, but if you have never written any comedy and don't know where to start, here are a few ideas to get you going.

Comedy is all about the **unexpected**. You walk your audience down a rosy path and then turn the other way—irony, opposites, silly juxtapositions of ideas or objects. "Saddle Oxfords and a Ford transmission." "Horseback riding and windows." Once you do that you have forced yourself away from *logic* and can now think of something "funny"! "Funny" is usually *illogical*. Keep a notebook of amusing ideas—just ideas: "We sell pizza and sport coats—only pepperoni and gold lamé!" Sounds stupid, and it is. Well, that goes in the book, exactly like that. And then one day, when I am writing a script, I will look at my list of ideas, and that may be the seed of a funny routine. I will probably toss it out and go to a different idea entirely, but the *premise* may make me think of something along those lines. That exact premise made me think of a different juxtaposition of dissimilar ideas. In one of my routines I mention, in passing, that "**I used to go to a combination gym and liquor store in Beverly Hills.**" And the comedic love story proceeds from that premise. It's silly! And I like silly. The other "first" idea, which was the catalyst that got me thinking in that direction, has never seen the light of day. And so it shouldn't! But you can see where a stupid idea can take you. Don't be afraid of stupid ideas!

So, there you have an introduction to writing yourself something to say onstage, even if you have never done that before. At least, that is how I began. And I write new stuff all the time. When you have a good, completed monologue—short or lengthy—memorize it and recite it over and over, while you are driving, when you are waiting for an appointment, or wherever, tweaking as you go. When I am not sure of some wording, I paraphrase the thought in a whole lot of different ways and speak the sentence out loud. Eventually, I say to myself, "How would Emile say that?" Make it something you could say to a friend when appropriate without thinking about it. Do it till it becomes a natural, short anecdote or story that you can keep in your repertoire. You will find that it will have many uses in life and will make you more confident onstage.

Chapter 30

SHOWTIME!

There's No Business like Show Business!

In a discussion of how to play in public, there are many component parts, all of which contribute to what we may call a satisfying performance for your audience. In this chapter are some suggestions and ideas gleaned from years of playing hundreds of concerts for thousands of people. Because we all know that the actual playing of the instrument is the most important thing we are doing, we sometimes forget to practice other parts of a performance, without which we do not come across in a "professional" manner; or worse, we may appear naïve or inexperienced. The following recommendations are designed to help you feel completely at ease onstage and to avoid distractions from the actual playing. Why are these ancillary discussions important? Because when you are sitting on the bench, **you want no surprises**.

We will be talking here about a performance in a recital hall, church, concert stage, or even your teacher's living room but *not a piano bar or club*, since those last two are more casual and usually don't require the same concert etiquette. However, the suggestions about familiarizing yourself with the performance surroundings are still valid.

Often, student recitals happen in rented spaces, churches, recital halls, auditoriums, or theaters within a school that the student is attending. So, the following are some facets of playing that appertain to the subject of *entertaining* an audience at any level—beginner to advanced. These are some of the issues that need to be taken into consideration so that we—*and the audience!*—can be at ease, confident that we have done all the preparatory work before we actually sit down at the piano.

In any professional contract, there is a "tech rider," which addresses a lot of these issues, but here we will talk about what you can do—even if this is your first public performance—to feel confident and stress-free and look like you know what you are doing in any situation where you are asked to play.

Let me be more specific. From time to time, we have all witnessed a truly brilliant performance (especially a classical one) by a fine pianist, but the artist appeared nervous, unsure, or uncomfortable walking onstage. Or, when he introduced the work he was about to play, we couldn't understand what he was saying; or he appeared uncomfortable when he took a bow, or there were long silences between pieces. In a classical recital, to this day, many artists still walk onstage, say nothing, and begin playing; and then, at the end of that piece, after an uncomfortable-looking bow, they—for no apparent reason—walk offstage, count to five, walk back on, say nothing, and begin the next piece of music. This is just odd and does not, in my estimation, contribute anything worthwhile to the performance. However, that format was standard practice when I was in college in music school; and now, *50 years later*, it is still happening. *(Dang! I just confessed to my advanced age!)* It has just never changed.

How this tradition began, I do not know, but Franz Liszt changed all that when he began to *talk* to the audience during his "musical soliloquies," which later came to be called "recitals." For some reason, we do not all follow that model. Well, for one thing, we are not all as charismatic as he was nor as gifted an entertainer.

That said, here are some *nonmusical* components of live performance that we need to explore. These are skills, like any other, that need to be rehearsed just like playing the piano does—except they are a lot easier to master.

So, what are some of these other ingredients that conspire to create a public performance that is more enjoyable and comfortable for the audience and yourself? Well, there are a few important things that you can do. I would like to bring to your attention some aspects of live performance that you may have considered but just did not pursue. These happen *before* the actual concert day if possible.

Arrival at the Venue: Honey, I'm Home!

First—and this is really important!—find out who your contact for the concert is, learn their name, and get their mobile number! Put that number into your phone or write it down way ahead of time. This may seem fairly obvious, but you might be surprised at how often you don't have that information when you need it. It could be your teacher; it might be a coordinator at the school. If you are a young student, then make sure that your parent has this information. *It is still your responsibility.* There is always someone who is overseeing the event, and you need to be able to reach that person at a moment's notice.

Second—and this is also often overlooked—if at all possible, visit the venue sometime (a day or more) before the concert. Walk around; investigate everything about it. For example, find out where you will park your car to "load in" and whether you will have to move your car to another spot *after* load-in. That is pretty common, even at churches. Your contact will tell you if there is a loading dock somewhere toward the side or back of the venue, which is often a more convenient place to bring in your concert clothes and anything else you may need. Find out where it is so you don't have to worry about it on the day or get anxious because you can't find a parking space. This is true whether it be a church, or a performing arts center, or even a person's house. There are parking restrictions in some neighborhoods.

Having found out *in advance* where you will park on the day of the performance, continue your preparations, ahead of the performance date if possible, by finding the person in charge of the actual room you will be performing in so that he or she can let you in (not surprisingly, the venue is probably locked). Familiarize yourself with the space you will be playing in. Look at the whole space attentively; find out how many seats it has. Walk to the stage; feel how the floor feels under your feet. Is it slippery? Are you then going to have to wear different shoes from the ones you had planned? Are there any uneven places on the floor between you and the piano? Are you afraid you might trip? Does the floor make noise or squeak when you walk? Will that make you self-conscious?

Look for the *exact* place where you will be walking ***from***. How long does it take to get from backstage (or side stage) to the piano? Practice the walk, back and forth, two or three times (or 10 times till you are comfortable) until you know exactly how long it takes, what sounds your shoes make, and whether there are any cables or other stuff in the way. Is it dark backstage, or are there obstacles in your path? If possible, ask the tech person to turn the lights the way they will be at the performance—house lights out, backstage and work lights out, but with the front lights that you will be staring into turned on. You may be surprised at how different the room and stage look when the lights are adjusted for the performance. Might there be a stage light shining directly in your eyes when you sit down to play? You will (almost always) be entering from stage right, as that way you can walk directly to the keyboard and not to the tail of the piano.

Make sure you are familiar with the terms "stage right," "stage left," "upstage," and "downstage" in case someone uses those terms. (This is relevant even if you are a very young student, around eight or 10 years old. Just learn them.)

"Stage right" is the right side of the stage from the performer's point of view, facing the audience. The opposite with "stage left." "Upstage" is toward the back of the stage, and "downstage" is toward the audience (again from the performer's point of view). "Centerstage" is just what it sounds like. The converse of these terms (from the audience perspective) is "*house* right" and "*house* left." Be familiar with these so you don't sound like a newbie, even if it is your first performance in a theater setting. If you are a teacher or parent of a young student, help them to learn these terms, even at a tender age. You may be asked where you are going to enter from or where you want the piano placed, things like that, even in a smaller venue, so these terms come in handy and give the impression (correctly) that you know what you are doing up there onstage. You want to make yourself as familiar with the space as possible so that at showtime there are no surprises.

That research done, the next task is to find out where you will be relaxing while awaiting your turn to play.

Getting to the Stage: Um...Where Am I?

Did you ever see the movie *This is Spinal Tap*? It's a mockumentary of a British heavy metal band in the 1980s. In one scene, they are in a huge concert hall about to perform, only they can't find their way from the dressing room to the stage. The maze of never-ending halls and staircases looks like the underbelly of the famous Paris Opera House in the musical *Phantom of the Opera!*

I don't want that to happen to you. Usually—even with nonprofessional performances—there is a place to hang out before the show to prepare yourself. It may be a dressing room, a waiting area, a "green room" (which is a kind of lounge usually supplied with refreshments and living room-type furniture), a practice space, a choir loft, or sometimes even a repurposed large closet!

Wherever it is, find your way to and from there and check with your contact so that you won't mistakenly be locked out once you leave the room. Many schools and churches have doors that lock automatically. How do I know? Never mind. Sometimes you need the maintenance department to set them to stay unlocked. I always keep a roll of gaffer tape (theater-quality duct tape) handy, so that, if necessary, I can tape the door latch so it cannot lock.

Rehearse the walk to and from your dressing room. **And find out where the restrooms are!** Public and private. Know how long your performance is, even if it is just one piece or song in a longer program. A tech person or the contact person is likely to ask you for that information. Be as precise as you can.

So that's a summary of prepping your yourself to get all the preshow, non-musical, but very essential, items out of the way.

Walking onto the Stage at Show Time: These Boots Were Made for *Walkin'*!

I have heard it said that whenever ballet legend Mikhail Baryshnikov stood onstage, before he even took his first step, he looked like an **exclamation point.** His proud posture, his intense gaze at the audience as though he was looking at *you personally,* and his complete and utter confidence and commanding presence all conspired to make you eagerly anticipate his first move. You knew he belonged there.

The first thing you want to do when you walk onstage is capture the audience's attention. How could they miss you, right? You're the only one there. They will obviously see you arrive. But how will they *perceive who you are?*

Have you ever noticed that when a person approaches the piano to sit down to play, you already form an idea of whether he knows what he is doing? Is he timid? Is he confident? Communicating with an audience begins before you even play the first note. Shy or timid body language sends a signal to the audience that you don't want to be there. They worry about you. They hope you aren't nervous. You can actually make *them* nervous on your behalf! The audience want you to do well, whether they know you personally or not.

It is body language, yes, but not artificial posturing, nor is it acting. It is the body language resulting from a comfort and certainty that is in turn derived from an understanding of the music you are going to play—confidence derived from focused, intelligent practice, from a complete—almost cavalier—familiarity with the instrument, and from a sincere *desire to entertain and move* the listener.

Watch a ballroom-dance couple or an ice skater walk out onto the floor. Before the first note of music is played, you perceive—*or do not*—confidence, elegance, grace, whatever before they make the first move. You can guess that a dancer is going to be wonderful before she even takes a step. When she walks up to her partner to begin a waltz, she has already captured your attention. You (subconsciously) think *"Wow! She must be really good!"* Her posture, her carriage, her sense of confidence, the carefully chosen gait with which she walks—it's a personal thing. Don't imagine that the actors you see walking the red carpet to the Oscars haven't practiced the pace of the walk, allowing enough time for photographers to take the perfect shot. They know how they look from each angle; they also know that any step they take of those 500 feet from the limo to the venue might appear on the front page of *People* magazine.

This is what your preparation is all for, after all. You have done your homework, both physical and—importantly—mental and psychological, so that you have now arrived at the enviable state of mind that you have worked so hard for: **you cannot wait to get onto that stage!** You are ready to perform. You have done the hard work, have practiced focusing your attention on the music and not on yourself, and now it is time to share what you have acquired through discipline, understanding, and dedication with an audience of people who are here to be entertained for a couple of hours. That is what we are talking about. So, give it all you've got!

Remember: 211 Degrees Is Just *Hot Water*

Why just give a lukewarm performance? *Mean* what you say musically! Now is a good time for me to mention that I grew up in an Italian American household. We Italians feel everything in high definition. We do nothing by halves, good or bad. I grew up that way. I remember when I was a kid, and my mom might ask me something like "How was lunch at school today?" I probably said something like *"That was the worst meal that ever existed in the history of the universe, including planets as yet undiscovered AND black holes,"* instead of, for example "I ... uh ... I didn't like the peas." It's just how we BE. We experience all of life through a magnifying glass. It might be annoying to some people ...

(but it makes for good opera).

Ready, Steady, Go!

You have arrived at the piano. You are ready to say your hellos or recite your carefully rehearsed, "spontaneous" welcome speech, and you are ready to play. But you notice that the bench is not exactly where you left it. Perhaps the piano tuner moved it or, if you are part of a program, the person before you adjusted it to her best position. Take your time to adjust the bench. Fold the music rack down if you are not using it. Take as much time as you need to be comfortable before you start to play. Don't feel embarrassed while you do this. You could talk to the audience while you are doing these mundane actions so that the atmosphere doesn't become uncomfortable. Check that you have what you need. Don't overthink it; just do all this with a nonchalant attitude, just as you would at home. You don't want to be halfway into the piece and think "Oh, the music rack is up; I forgot to close it down," or "The bench is way too low!" All of these items should have been taken care of well before the concert started, but sometimes some of them are not done for one reason or another or might change in between performances, so now is the time to check them off your mental list—*before* you play.

 On rare occasions, the piano lid has been down when I walked onto the stage, and I have had to lift it up (with my back to the audience, of course). So, what did I do? I just lifted it up and said something dumb like "I gave the staff the day off today" or "I have to do everything around here!" Or "Have you any idea how much a piano lid weighs? Sheesh! I'm glad I went to the gym this morning!" Or "Be sure not to leave any programs on the floor because after the concert I have to sweep up."

Have the attitude that "it ain't no big thing." Be sure everything is "right" before you start to play. You'll be glad you did (and so will your audience because you have put them at ease.)

I always keep a paper program in the piano (because I am too lazy to memorize it), so now is the time to make sure any notes you put into the piano are now in a place where you can see them while seated on the bench. I always have a freshly starched handkerchief in there as well—just in case. I also keep another handkerchief in my coat or pants pocket.

Side note: If you cough or sneeze (heaven forbid!), don't be too self-conscious. Maybe say something like "Excuse me! I must be allergic to pianos! Bummer!" or something of your own invention. I always have a few (well-rehearsed) "spontaneous" lines ready in case of an unexpected interruption to the flow of the evening, like a phone ringing. ("If that's for me, tell them I'm busy.") Or a person sneezing. ("Bless you!") Or a siren outside. ("There's my ride!") Whatever …

Once you have checked everything and introduced the first piece, sit down to the instrument, feeling completely relaxed and ready to go. You love your audience, and they love you. And you haven't yet played a note.

In my show, I almost always start off with humor. I began that practice long ago to put myself—and, by extension, my audience—at ease. They know they don't have to sit up straight and behave. They can even cross their legs if they like! There are numerous examples online of entertainers talking to an audience in every style. I encourage you to listen—from the viewpoint of a *detective*—to actors you admire; watch them on talk shows and seriously study how they do what they do. Figure it out. Find out how you can improve your own stage presence; put this into the category of a skill that you must acquire or improve upon, and you will find it very fulfilling. And your audience will be very grateful for the invisible hard work you have done. I promise.

Once you have hooked their attention, you need to keep it from the get-go. From the first few seconds you want to hold it and give them an experience that they *want* to remember and *will* remember.

The Actual Performance: Are We There Yet?

Not quite.

The gift that keeps on giving—if you don't take it back!

A final word of advice before you begin to play. You are about to give the audience a gift. Maybe you begin to have doubts about it, silently. "I have this thing I want to give you. But what if you don't like it?" Suppose you buy someone a book for her birthday. You choose a Tom Clancy thriller. You give it to her. While she is opening the gift, you think "I should have got her John Grisham." Don't ruin the gift by saying to her, "I should have got you *The Firm*." The person who receives the gift **wants to love it.** Your audience is awaiting their gift from you. Don't spoil it by apologizing, even mentally, while you are giving it. Just give them the gift and assume they will love it. (Besides, you are not supposed to be looking inward! Remember?)

Another note on being comfortable onstage—when you have a choice, **don't perform your most difficult piece.** Wait till it's easy. Play pieces that you are comfortable with. Bottom line—you ALWAYS want to be perfectly at ease onstage, ALWAYS. You do not want to dread the next piece. Why do that to yourself *if you have a choice?*

With music you can "get away with" a few missed notes. But you don't want to put yourself in that worrisome place. So, do you *ever* get to perform it (your most challenging piece)? Yes. You wait until it is no longer your "hardest trick"; when it becomes just part of your repertoire. You're always working on something more difficult. No one but you knows whether it was difficult or not; they just know they enjoyed it.

As a *professional* pianist, because I get to choose the repertoire that I am going to learn or play in concert, I often weigh how much practice it's going to take to learn a new piece against what musical goal I hope to accomplish. Some of my easiest-to-perform pieces of music (or magic effects) get the most wonderful response. So, the deal is don't make yourself uncomfortable. If you really want to play the tune by a certain deadline, then practice your butt off. But don't perform an "impressive" tune before it's ready. **I've done it and messed up, and I felt stupid.** *(Since I am used to feeling stupid in front of a crowd, it wasn't so bad, but it could adversely affect a man of lesser inner strength.)* So *do* play it for your friends about a hundred times—whenever you get the chance—but before you perform it for strangers, i.e., friends you haven't met yet.

"Gosh! Look at The Time!": Don't Overstay Your Welcome

I don't like to brag, but I remember one particular performance when at the end, I got **a walking ovation!** I think the audience was so elated by the performance that they couldn't wait to get home and tell their friends!

At least that's how I interpreted it ...

You get the point. Don't "leave 'em wanting less."

Every type of venue is different—a concert hall, a church service, a casual party, a cocktail lounge, or a cabaret setting, on and on. Notice your surroundings and be flexible. So, when you are at a party and someone asks you to play, it's okay to play a *very short* version of *one* of your special arrangements. If they want more, they will ask for more, so you can then play another *short* tune (three minutes or so). Just know your audience and your location. I do a two-hour show (with intermission) in a performing arts center but about a three-minute tune when asked to do one at a party.

That said, here are a few words about the frame of mind you should aim for when you are performing specifically in a concert setting where you are the main attraction: **do exactly what you prepared in the practice room.** Some people say to themselves, during the performance, "Well, I'll just change a fingering, add a touch more *rubato*, play a little faster, or harder …blah-blah."

Nope. All that should have happened in the practice room. When you get up there, fully prepared, do exactly what you prepared. Yes, you could probably do it a little differently or "better"—*but not today*. Once onstage, do the **normal**. Don't change anything on the spot. You'll save yourself a lot of heartache.

"Say Goodnight, Gracie"

When you have played your last piece, it is time to take your final bow. Once again, this is a *skill*, be it ever so humble, that should be emulated from people you have watched online or learned from your teacher, but it must be rehearsed! How you bow is up to you because there are all sorts of bows: the "ta-da!" bow, the acrobat bow (big hand and arm gestures like you just got off a tight rope), the curtsy, the humble nod, or the gentle tilt of the head.

For example, when I have just played "Clair de Lune," my bow is *slow*, a little deep, respectful, and gentle, standing in front of the bench, probably with my left hand on the piano case (a classical recital style), allowing the audience to take as much time as they need to acknowledge the performance before I start the introduction to the next piece—very unlike the "ta-da!" bow after a novelty piece.

The main thing is to look (and *be*!) comfortable in your bow. Practice in front of a mirror and then a friend. You will feel silly at first but keep on doing it until you get over feeling silly. A bow is not a natural thing for us Westerners to do in our everyday lives, as it is in some cultures, so we need to practice it. Be gracious or showy or silly, but be sincere. A bow is saying "Thank you for listening to what I had to say." Make sure you "say" your bow in such a way that they feel that they have had a chance to fully acknowledge you for what you have just given them. Don't cut the applause short by coming out of the bow too soon and going into your next monologue or piece of music.

It Ain't over till It's Over

After the concert, whether it be a student recital, a solo performance, or an afternoon salon performance, it's time to mingle. Remember that you are still "onstage." If you meet and greet people, always be gracious, as you are still making an impression as a "celebrity"—even if you are a student. If you did not play your best that evening, ***don't tell on yourself***, let it be your little secret. You can work on it tomorrow. If someone says, "Oh, I loved your rendition of the Brahms *Intermezzo*," don't say, "Well, it wasn't my best today. I can play it a whole lot better than that." When you do something like that, it tells the person that they cannot discern good playing from bad. It is an insult, and the person goes away feeling a little stupid. Just say, "Thank you. I am so glad you enjoyed it." Treat every comment as what it is—a sincere thank-you for what they enjoyed about the gift you gave them. Never apologize. That comes later with your teacher, close friends, or other mentor.

What Is "Charisma" and Where Can I Get Some? (Hint: You Can't)

As I have said, onstage you want to come across as self-confident. *The audience needs that from you.* There is "self-confidence," and there is "self-esteem." Self-confidence is about skill. You have worked hard at perfecting your craft, and you know *what* you can do. Self-esteem is about integrity. You know *who* you are, skillful or not. Onstage that comes across as being comfortable in front of all those people. You are not trying to prove anything. You are just enjoying being up there, ready to give the audience a gift of music. The general allure that some people seem to unwittingly possess is what we call "charm," and I think it comes from that person's genuine love and caring for others. What we call "charisma" comes from somehow connecting with people in a spiritual and visceral way. You might define the word "charisma" as "dynamic charm" or "charm on steroids"—which is also something known as "personal magnetism." Charm is engaging someone's attention and holding it as you tell them a story while loving them at the same time. Some people call that collection of characteristics charisma. Charisma is not a skill. Since you can't learn it, there's not a thing you can do to become charismatic. That's a judgment for other people to make based on how your personality affects them. So, since you can't learn it, what has this to do with piano performance?

Nothing.

Everything.

"Nothing" because you cannot say to yourself, "I am going to cast a magic spell over these people. I will be charismatic!" That is something for them to determine.

"Everything" because you can develop in yourself an *honest* feeling of love for your audience—that they are your new friends, and therefore you treat them that way. And you are excited about what you have to give them. Then you leave it at that. I believe that genuinely *loving people* is interpreted onstage (and probably in life too) as *"charm"* or *"charisma."* You can't fake being kind. You can't fake loving your audience. If they think you are charming, great. If they think you are charismatic, great. That is not up to you. It's like asking for a standing ovation. You can't. *(Unless it's your house and you are playing a free concert for your mom's birthday party with all her best friends there, and you didn't put any chairs out.)*

The good news is that it doesn't matter whether someone describes you as "charismatic" or not. It really doesn't. But what *does* matter is being kind, thoughtful, empathetic, interesting, and sincerely remembering that what you are doing onstage is all about making the audience glad they came to the performance.

"Without Whom None of This Would Be Possible"

The concert and meet and greet are now over, but the evening isn't. As you load out and leave the building, be kind and considerate to the crew: the maintenance people, the tech crew, and the ushers; don't forget to especially thank the presenter who scheduled the show in the first place. Thank all of them. This is not insincere. It is recognizing the fact that—literally—you cannot have a performance without the talents, efforts, and contributions of all these people. And those people will genuinely appreciate your acknowledgement. It is never too early to get into this habit. You can instruct your child to do that when she is six years old in her first performance in the teacher's living room. He can thank his teacher for teaching him that piece that he loves to play, thank his dad for helping him tie his tie; she can thank Mom for helping her pick out a dress for the recital and thank the person who made the lemonade and set up the chairs in the living room. And while it may be a deliberate action at first, you will quickly realize that this is something you *ought* to do, and more than finding out that people are grateful that you recognized their contributions, you will begin to develop a holistic view of any type of performance. You will know that when you go to a party and are asked to sit down to play that someone made the area as lovely as possible, had the piano tuned, and rearranged the furniture so the guests could comfortably listen to the "impromptu" concert that you both prepared in such detail! So much effort behind the scenes conspires to make an event look effortless. Just think about when you have been in the background of an event and not the star. Doesn't it feel good when someone acknowledges you for baking the cookies, running to the store at the last minute to get some more ice, or putting away the folding chairs and cleaning up after the evening's festivities?

As you load out, and as you leave the building, be courteous, polite, and friendly *(including while you are driving away—other drivers will recognize you)*. People will see you and know who you are. Some guests will inevitably be staying at the same hotel as you. The time to relax will be when you are back home or in your room at the hotel.

So, there you have it. Some things to make you so comfortable that you will relish your next performance, knowing that you have taken care of all the *other* stuff—both before and after the concert—ahead of time, and delight in the mental freedom that allows you to have your attention focused only on the music. Then, unhampered by nonmusical considerations and having all of your skills and abilities *literally* at your fingertips, you can concentrate on soaring to new musical heights because you can now

play it like you mean it.

Chapter 31

ARE YOU SURE YOU EVEN *WANT* ONE?

"Can I Make a Living at It?"

To begin, this is a discussion about whether or not you actually *want* to consider a career in music and then some advice on "how to." You are a pianist and are thinking about making commercial music your career. Wonderful! I speak from extensive experience when I say that it is a great lifestyle that I love and enjoy every single day.

Although we all mostly start from the same place educationally, and that is the classical grounding in playing piano, there are really just two basic directions in which to go for a musician: classical and "everything else." For the sake of ease, let's call "everything else" commercial music. The two are not mutually exclusive, but they have different requirements, and people who play one style often move in different circles from those who play the other.

When considering a career, teaching is an obvious profession to look at. I have a deep respect for those of you who have chosen teaching as a vocation. All three of my sisters and several nieces and nephews have pursued that fulfilling and rewarding lifestyle. If it weren't for remarkable people like them and you, I would not enjoy the performing career that I have today. Maybe you want to spend your working life in academia, teaching at the university level and doing occasional concerts, another exciting and gratifying aspect of that career choice in the classical field.

Then there are those of us who choose to make a living performing commercial music, and that is what I shall talk about because that is what I know. We get to play and record all the "other" wonderful music that surrounds us daily in shops, restaurants, and bars—and, yes, in elevators and grocery stores. We also get to perform live in clubs, festivals, and performing arts centers. There are numerous options available to you if you go down this route to share your music with the world on a daily basis to make a happy person happier or to relieve a person who is undergoing an emotional trial. That said, how do we embark on this career path and still pay the rent?

People routinely tell me just how lucky they think I am to be doing something I really love. And it is true. I am very fortunate indeed. By contrast, many people have a profession or a job that they enjoy well enough. They meet nice people or make a good living, but they feel that something is missing. They are not fulfilled by what they are doing day in and day out. Some cannot wait to retire. I, on the other hand, can't wait to do a concert on my 100th birthday. You get what I mean. Easier said than done? Yup. But doable? Yup.

There is a very simple way to resolve this dilemma. Here's the normal (sincere but impractical) answer, one that we have *all* heard*!*

"Follow your heart and the rest will work itself out."

Um—or it won't!

But at least you will have followed your heart, and you can look in the mirror and honestly say, years later, "I followed my heart." Being able to say that is, sadly, rare but is truly a boon and a blessing especially when you are experiencing adversity. But it doesn't always pay the rent. So, here's the much, *much* longer version.

If you are sincerely even *considering* a career in music, then you must really like playing music every single day. If you can be totally honest with yourself, then I am willing to bet you already know whether that is true or not for you. There is only *one* factor that is making almost any career decision of this nature into an unresolvable dilemma, and that is **money**. Yes, we all know this, but really look at it. The question is probably *not* "If I could do anything I wanted, would I choose to spend my lifetime doing music?" (Because the answer is probably a resounding "yes!") The **real** question, then, is "Can I make a living at it?" Money is a problem. Money is *the* problem.

Well, *that's good news* because it simplifies things a whole lot. Because, sadly, money is *always* the problem—for everyone in *any* career! And for many people, there are *two* problems—not making enough money *and* not knowing what they want to do for a living! Wouldn't you prefer to have just *one* problem?

So, the following discussion is for the musician who wants to make a living as a player of some kind of commercial music. It can be a difficult path, as there is no large organization to which you can ally yourself or your band, nor is there a "corporate ladder" to climb. You are pretty much on your own.

As a pianist, however, you are ahead of the pack because there are far more opportunities for playing solo than there are for a player of any other instrument. I have nearly always worked on my own, first as a cocktail pianist and much later in performing arts centers as a concert artist doing my own one-man shows (more about that later). I am telling you this because I want you to know that there is always a way to make your dreams a practical reality. It just takes imagination, research, and hard work.

Now consider this. How badly do you want to play music for people? Are you willing to sometimes live paycheck to paycheck doing what you *want*? Are you willing to start out with odd jobs like, for example, being a waiter or waitress, a receptionist, or cashier to make ends meet so you can do your music when the opportunity arises?

If you truly want to be a professional musician, there is always a way. You just have to be willing to starve a little, take all sorts of other work, and do it *happily* because it solves a problem. I spent several years living from scary day to scary day wanting to have music as a profession but not knowing how I would pay the rent. It was horrible! But I finally solved that ridiculous situation by ... um ... ***working!*** I worked as a house painter, drywall installer with a construction company, and janitor—whatever I could do. And what a relief it was to know that I could eat that day! There is *always* something you can do. Always. If that's what allows you to follow your dream, then that is a *gift*, not a burden.

So...Should I Get a "Day Job?"

Hmmm ... let me think about that. **YES!**

I have heard people say things like "If I take a 'day job,' it means I have given up on my dream." No, it means quite the opposite. It means that you are willing to do *whatever it takes to **achieve your dream***. It means you are responsible, determined, and *practical*. You should be applauded by your peers. You are making it possible for yourself to pursue your dream. Know that. The day job is a *blessing* that you give yourself. And a side note here: day jobs are just that—*day jobs*. Most of your playing jobs happen in the evening. You can handle two jobs. It's what many people do anyway.

At least in my experience, the fact that *money was coming in* was such an incredible relief that the time I *did* spend at the piano was a bonus and a pure joy because it was worry-free. Besides that, I enjoyed—or just decided to enjoy—whatever job I was doing, thankful that the job was making it possible for me to eat and have a roof over my head. I was grateful to have a job as a janitor. I am not kidding. Truly. When you don't have *basic-need* worries, then your mind is free to create your music while you are working to find your dream job. Suffering does not make you a better artist, no matter what the novels say. It just makes you suffer.

Here is another way to look at this conversation. If you are bemoaning the fact that you have to wait tables or flip burgers at a fast-food diner in the small town where you grew up, please recognize that they have table-waiting and burger-flipping jobs all over America **and the world**—even in exotic places. You could be flipping burgers in Cozumel, waiting tables on Hilton Head Island, or housekeeping on a cruise ship or a private yacht. If you think your current "make-ends-meet" job is boring or awful, remember that those very same "boring or awful" jobs can be had in a resort town at the beach, in the mountains, in the desert, or on the French Riviera. Anyone can fill out an application for international jobs. I am speaking from experience. Think *way* outside the box.

One of my favorite other-than-music jobs was when I worked for two years in a jewelry store in St. Thomas, Virgin Islands. (*The **US** Virgin Islands*—no passport needed) It was just a "day job to get by," *but it was in paradise!* And I learned a lot about beautiful watches and jewelry. Puerto Rico and Hawaii are part of the good ol' USA. So is Alaska! Want to go there? Get a roommate or two to help with the rent. There is always a way to start from where you are so you can get on the road to where you want to be. You could be a personal assistant to someone who needs one. Maybe work for the maintenance company that services a recording studio, get to know the engineers or some of the people recording there, and eventually exchange your work for some studio time to record your first album.

One of my hobbies is performing sleight of hand magic. For a short while when I was living in LA, I became—quite by chance—the sometime *driver* for an elderly (famous) magician who could no longer drive himself. I loved it; I learned a lot, and I made a few bucks. As I recall, *none* of these out-of-the-ordinary jobs were on any of the aptitude tests I took.

So, let's assume you know that you want to do music as a lifetime career and that—at least for now—you have to do other jobs. **That is not bad news**. It's *good* news because you can pay the rent and put food on the table.

Look around you. Start asking people a good deal older than you if their entire careers were happy and carefree. I am willing to bet that 90 percent of them will have horror stories to tell. That's just how life can be.

For most people, ups and downs are a part of growing, learning, and finding their way till they can do what they really want. Perhaps you are among the people (like me) who have always known what they want to do with their lives. We never really considered any other possibility. I was so sure about that, as were my sisters, that I never knew that many people entering college did not yet know what they wanted to do for a lifetime career. Later, I found out I was just one of a lucky few. But if you *do* know that music is for you, that gives you a running start because you can devote your time in college to acquiring all the skills and knowledge you need for your eventual career, instead of trying out this course and that to see whether you can spend a lifetime doing it.

Say "goodbye," starving artist.

Can You Make a Good Living as a Musician Performing Pop Music?

You bet you can! You just have to be creative, open minded, and adventurous. Success does not depend on the field you are in but rather whether it is the field that you *want* to be in. You can make money at anything if you really get creative.

Side note: A word about my philosophy of getting a job playing piano—I moved around a good deal in my young adult years, usually without a plan *and without a job to go to. That means that as soon as I arrived in the new town or city and began to set up my new life, I had to find out what work opportunities were available to me. After college, I lived in the Virgin Islands, England, Denver, Los Angeles, and finally, Greenville, SC, where I now live. In each of these places, I found a playing job **after** I arrived.*

During many of these moves, people said to me, "There are no music jobs in [that town]." Or: "The economy is not doing well right now; you will have a hard time finding any job in entertainment."

There are numerous considerations to be made and genuine facts to be found out that may be statistically accurate about a place but not necessarily encouraging or helpful. I never listened to them. My view was—and I encourage you to consider—this:

*"I only need ONE JOB. There only has to **be** one job. I don't care about the market, the part of the country I am in, or how other industries are doing. I am **one person** who needs **one job**."*

That viewpoint has never failed me.

I am not suggesting that you decide right this minute whether to make music a career or not. I am telling you it is not a hard decision. It really isn't. If your goal is to make a lot of money in life—*and that is a perfectly laudable goal*—then you should look at all the various options that are likely to produce that result. You talk to counselors, friends, and successful people you know and find out what's out there. Then it is the trial and error of finding out, of those options, what you are really gifted at or what you would be willing to do for the next 40 years. Maybe you become a corporate executive or enter the legal profession, something you are good at that is famous for producing large amounts of income, and keep the piano playing as a wonderful hobby. Maybe, if nothing seems to fit, you have to create a business of your own and work for yourself. The thrust of this thesis is don't wait for something outside yourself to "kind of work for you" for a job. You may have to do that at first. Most of us do. But keep looking for *your comfort zone or happy place* and find out how to do something that lets you get there and stay there. The best job *(for you)* in the world! Making lots of money at something you are good at so you can travel, do what you like, and enjoy a prosperous lifestyle may be so rewarding that you are quite content having music as a hobby. There is nothing wrong with that.

I know someone will say, "Yeah, but I would like to only work a few hours a week and lie on the beach or play tennis the rest of the time." Well, guess what? That is also a possibility. Some people do that. Have you ever read the book *The 4-hour Work Week* by Tim Ferriss? Look it up. Maybe it is for you. Maybe you are a day trader on Wall Street. Maybe you are a minimalist, have a "tiny" 700-foot home, and like walking dogs for people for a living (no pressure and no homework involved). Keep thinking everywhere but "normal" places. Be creative!

Maybe you will write a bestselling novel or textbook, then spend the rest of your life on the beach teaching people to paddleboard by day and bartend at night. I know (because I lived there) that there are some people doing exactly that in St. Thomas to this day—and probably in a thousand other places that I've never heard of—and loving their off-the-grid lives. Maybe you play piano in a nightclub in one of these places. Maybe you become an internationally famous rock star or the best lounge pianist in Bali. Don't limit yourself to the normal career paths—unless they suit you to a tee.

My dad's mantra was **"Don't be a statistic. If everyone is doing it, *do something else.*"** I like it. And I have always done that. Something else. Yes, it has worked out pretty well. *Except maybe that time when everyone was buying stock in Sony Walkman and I bought RCA eight-track players—oops!* But apart from that unpleasantness, it has worked pretty well!

Chapter 32

THE BIG DECISION!

Yeah, but What If I TRULY DON'T KNOW What I Want to Do for the Rest of My Life?

I have a little exercise for anyone who is not sure of what they want to do for a career. It's my own sort of aptitude test and has nothing whatever to do with a standard career test. This is not a "how-to" but an effort to look somewhere other than where you may have been programmed (subconsciously) to look.

Instead of (as in aptitude tests) trying to find out what your strengths and weaknesses are based on your personality, education, and skills, try this.

Make yourself a list of questions like the following (as many as you can think of) that have *nothing* to do with the actual job skills, requirements, training, or education but *everything* to do with having a *happy living and working environment*, finding out who you are, and therefore loving your life. Because

how you spend your *days* is how you spend your *life*!

Here we go!

When you wake up in the morning, where would you like to be?

What's outside your bedroom window?

What do you see when you look out the window of your workspace? Big city? Small town? Farm? Mountains? Beach?

What aromas would you like to smell as you wake up? Coffee? Fresh air? The smells of an alive, exciting city?

What sounds greet you as you wake up? Birds chirping? Farm animals? Subways rumbling? Horns honking?

What *time* would you like to get up? *(Any answer, including "noon," is OK.)*

What kind of clothes do you want to wear to work?

Would you prefer to work from *home* in your pajamas? Jeans? Business suit? Casual elegance?

Do you like parties? Like to dress up?

Would you prefer to work at a big office with lots of people or alone in your studio?

After work do you want to hang with friends at your favorite watering hole? Or go home by yourself and watch TV? Maybe quietly read a book?

Do you like music in the background all the time? Silence when you are working?

Do you like keeping up with the news? Or never want to know what's going on in the world?

Would you mind working 80-hour weeks? Two jobs if necessary? Are you a workaholic?

How many people do you want to see in a workday? One? Dozens? Nobody?

Do you like meeting new people? Prefer to be left alone?

Do you like strangers? Or do you have just one or two best friends?

Do you love everybody?

Do you like challenges in your daily work? Like *no* challenges, just a job?

How about working just to pay the bills, and taking weekends off?

Would you love to be your own boss? Hate to be your own boss?

Are you a sports person?

Do you want to be in a quiet (library-type) environment?

Do you love to travel?

Do you hate to travel?

On and on. *Ask yourself and answer everything you can think of that has nothing to do with the actual job.* Then do an honest evaluation and find out what you **default** to!

"If I had my druthers …" I would live every day/most of the time/some of the time/occasionally/*never* in this sort of environment, with this sort of work schedule, and so on **but**—important during this exercise—**never thinking practically** or about "where does my money come from?" **Not now!**

This is a soul exercise; this is about finding out who you *really* are. So keep money out of it. No "now-I'm-supposed-to-answer-this-responsibly" responses. There are—*literally*—no "wrong" answers. One example of a "right" answer could be: "I never want to do any work my whole life, and I want to eat licorice every day, win the lottery, and be rich and stupid." No one else will read this, so concentrate on being honest with yourself so that you don't defeat the purpose of the exercise. Got that?

Great. Then, having done that exercise ad nauseam, by all means—***get a job of any kind!*** The psychological relief it gives you is immeasurable, knowing that the creature comforts are looked after.

When you know what your *preferred working environment* is, you can start doing research to see what kinds of jobs are available that have those time schedules, challenges, days off, locations, and all those requirements of yours.

You will find out:

1. So *that's* who I am! I feel like I know myself so much better than I ever have. I am not secretly feeling guilty for maybe not wanting to make music a full-time profession. Now I have some options that I never considered before.

2. Now that the basics are under control because I *have* a job, I can spend all my free time investigating, contemplating, researching, asking around, and practicing my music. Now, how do I put together all the parts of my working environment that I now know I want in my life for the next 40 years?

You may find out after all that, that although you **thought** you wanted— or *should* want— music as a career, after close inspection, maybe you really don't anymore. Music may become an enthusiastic hobby. **That is okay too.** You can now just enjoy your music and go about finding your *real* career. When you do find out your "default" place, you may (or probably will) have to go to school or do some sort of training for it. But that will be a joy because now you are not floundering around wondering what to do when you grow up.

If, on the other hand, the very thought of doing something other than your dream of playing music makes you feel depressed and resigned to your fate, well then, you really have no choice. You *must* follow your dream. So good luck with your soul-searching. There is no right answer. But there is an *honest* answer, and that is the one you want.

Look, you only pursue the arts because you *have* to. It's not a sure thing; it's not a guaranteed money-maker. If you don't have an **"I-must-do-this!"** feeling, then I suggest keeping it as a wonderful hobby.

One more thing—whether you are in college or not, TAKE A BUSINESS COURSE! I wish I had. I think *everyone* should be required to take at least an introductory business class in high school or college. Some of the finest musicians I know are starving—not from lack of talent or hard work—from their *lack of business skills*. Do it! Go to a business school near you right now and sign up. That's a ***for-sure***.

I hope you like long-winded answers!

But you did ask.

Chapter 33

GETTING DOWN TO BUSINESS

Let's continue with the assumption that you have decided to pursue a career in music. If it is truly what you desire in your heart, then there are many, many things you can do with piano, short of having a concert career. Besides the jobs I have had that were mentioned in an earlier chapter, I have played for silent films (No! Not when they originally came out! Sheesh! I'm not *that* old!), played for retro-vaudeville shows including melodrama plays, accompanied a stage hypnotist, played on other musicians' recording sessions and for acting classes and dance auditions, accompanied vocal coaches, backed improv groups, and played with bands of many genres from jazz to calypso, to rock and folk music. I did all of this before recording or performing my own concerts. You **can** find a way to survive while you pursue your dream job.

If you haven't begun your adventure into marketing your music, a good place to start is DIY Musician (Do It Yourself Musician—a CD Baby service), where you will find a wealth of information on how to monetize your music. Really, today there is an inexhaustible supply of free information on this subject on social media, online tutorials, and industry-sponsored blogs. It is never-ending. When you submit your music to CD Baby, for example, they distribute it to numerous online platforms—some that you (or I) may never have heard of—that stream your music worldwide. All genres are catered for, from rap, to electronic, to experimental, to classical. You just need to put your thinking cap on and happily do the work that has to be done *away from the piano*. I know, I know—you would prefer to be sitting at the piano. Me too.

All that said, caveat emptor:
You have to have a Judy!

Many times, I have been asked how I "did it" (got from piano bars to the concert stage). Well, that is a long story. And, importantly, *my* path from cocktail piano to the concert stage is ***ancient history*** because the music industry has changed so much since I began recording in 1990. And I had a great deal of help. For those of you who are interested, I'll give you a summary of what we did because it may be helpful to find out about another person's journey, even if it is not one you can follow today. I have always found it enlightening to learn how someone achieved their goal of a successful, long-lasting career while starting from a modest beginning. Together, *my* Judy and I were able to construct a thriving career using the tools and methods that were available to us at the time, starting from scratch. Here is an overview of what we did; after this brief synopsis, I will be more specific.

I have always chosen to be an independent artist. Back in 1990, that was not a common thing. Today indies thrive, and this fact is a wonderful game-changer. But in the early '90s, there was no widely available Internet; we were recording on two-inch reel-to-reel tape and exclusively selling hard copy music (cassettes first and then CDs). Much later, when the industry moved to selling music through digital platforms, we moved with it. We morphed the business model as the marketplace evolved. We set up a website as soon as that was feasible. We changed our newsletter marketing from hard copy to digital. When streaming came along, we were quick to submit my music to iTunes (an arduous process at the time) and soon found out that the only way to get accepted as an indie was to go through CD Baby or other well-known industry distributors. Through CD Baby, our music has been moving to new platforms as they arise. You must keep up with market trends and new opportunities to get your music out into the world. In many ways, it is a hundred times easier—and far cheaper!—today than it was then. With distribution now primarily digital, there is very little CD manufacturing, so less printing of promotional materials, and, consequently, a lot lower costs of shipping. But the basic business principles still apply. No matter how the structure of the industry may change, all of these elements still have to be taken care of.

A Short Digression: Paradigm Shift

How to do that? Well, throughout this book, I am encouraging you to *start by changing a paradigm in your thinking*. Many musicians and other artists (including me) have held the viewpoint that business is one of those things that "non-artists" do and that business sense is just not part of our personality. We think that somehow the business end will take care of itself. Unfortunately, that is not the case.

The particular shift in your approach (your "aha!" moment) that I am asking you to embrace is "I get it! Music, *like everything else on this planet*, *truly is a business, and I shouldn't be fighting the fact that it **is** a business.*" It makes no sense, and wastes a lot of time, to object to a fact of life. Really understand that viewpoint! When you *genuinely* get into that frame of mind, you will see that the work that you do away from the piano is actually very valuable and can even be enjoyable because now you are making it possible to actually get your music out into the world, bring enjoyment to others, and fulfill yourself as an artist. Don't just pay it lip service; actually *believe* it because it is the path to financial freedom. More importantly, it is also the path to creative and emotional freedom. You can create and produce far more when you are not bending under the weight of worrying about paying the rent. From this moment forward, begin the shift in understanding that music—*your* music—is a business like any other and demands care and maintenance, just like your house, your car, and your pet. When you finally make a pact with yourself that "it is what it is," you won't be doing the business activities begrudgingly but with optimism, knowing that every hour spent in that enterprise is bringing you closer to your goal.

Many of you will say, "I already know that music is a business. I just am not a business person." I am sorry if you are not a "businessperson." Neither am I. But you may have to become one if you want to survive. I will share with you how we "did it," recognizing that everyone is different and, therefore, everyone's path is different. However, it may open your eyes to what must occur for you to create and maintain a successful career of your own design. What follows is an overview of how we got from "hither to yon," with the good news that it can be done. First things first:

You Have to Have a Judy

OK, so what's a "Judy"? She is a manager, a CEO, an overseer, a career path designer, a bookkeeper, an organizer, and a businesswoman. If you're lucky, she will run your whole business. A Judy will suggest what songs to play, how much you should charge for your services, what subjects you can talk about onstage, what subjects *never* to discuss onstage, and gently remind you which activities (like rehearsing) are more important than watching football. She will keep you producing instead of goofing off.

And she will keep you humble.

In short: you have to have a Judy.

Yes, Judy is my wife.

But she's also a metaphor. (I hope she doesn't mind being a metaphor.)

You have to have one. You don't have to *marry* one, or be related to one, or even hire one. You could be your *own* Judy. **But there *must* be one.** Caveat: you need someone you trust *(he/she will be in charge of running your business, including—importantly—finances)*, someone who you know has your best interests at heart and is able to tell you what you need to hear, not a yes-man.

Sadly, most artists (even great ones, including Van Gogh) didn't have a Judy. (Well, Vincent had his brother, Theo, who tried to be his manager but sold only one painting during Vincent's lifetime. History tells us that he was a wonderful, well-meaning, devoted brother, but he was no Judy.)

So, let's have a look at exactly what *my* Judy did for our business back in the day. At the beginning, we followed the independent route. We never tried to get a record deal—or even an agent—for many years, although at the time, that was the more tried-and-true way to go. We have just always liked being our own bosses and being in charge of our own destiny. That way, if we win, we congratulate ourselves; if we lose, we have no one else to blame. What follows is a general outline of what we did to create a very successful career path for ourselves.

To Begin: LA 1980

When Judy and I met and got married (well, not just like *that*—we got to *know* each other first! *Good grief!*), I was doing all sorts of playing jobs in LA with no plan or even a *thought* of a plan of how I might make things better. I just wanted to make sure I had a job playing piano—some job, *any* playing job. During six of those years in LA, I played piano at the Comedy Store, besides playing the other types of occasional gigs that I mentioned earlier.

In 1980, Judy knew something about the music business. She had always loved music and had many friends who were musicians, recording engineers, or band members; she had taken several courses in music business at UCLA several years before we met. But the music industry was evolving, so by the time she started putting our business together, much later, in the early '90s, it was a very different environment from what it had been when she had studied the basics. We got married in LA in 1983. As I mentioned, I was working at the Comedy Store, and we got by. In 1983, we moved to South Carolina, and I found a steady job as a cocktail pianist in a high-end dinner club called The City Club in Greenville, SC, where we now live. South Carolina at that time was fairly insular, musically speaking. You can imagine it was not like LA! And in 1990, the Internet was brand new and not widely available; there was no one to talk to or learn from. Judy decided to concentrate on the business side of the music industry, so she started from the ground up, educating herself exclusively with books, in particular one called *This Business of Music* by M. William Krasilovsky, which she read cover to cover. To this day she credits that exhaustive text with helping her to map out a viable career path for both of us. Incidentally, that book, now on its 10th edition, is still available. I highly recommend it.

One day while I was playing at the dinner club, which I did for about six years, one of my "regulars" mentioned that he saw some music being offered for sale in a gift shop and that it was a similar genre to mine. He thought that I should investigate that marketplace. I'll tell you about that more specifically later.

Well, I mentioned to Judy offhandedly that I thought it would be nice to be making a living selling recordings (on cassette at the time) instead of playing at the restaurant. Well, be careful what you say around *your* Judy because they will take the ball and run with it. *Immediately.* And she did. The only trouble was we didn't have any recordings to sell. So, the first step was, of course, to record an album. But how? At that time, we had no recording contract, no studio, no record deal, and certainly no funds for the project.

So, What to Do? What to Do?

Since we had no money to work with, that same very creative patron and friend from the dinner club suggested that we presell 10 cassettes at $10 each to 20 patrons in order to pay for the recording session *and* the manufacture of the cassettes. It was a sort of "GoFundMe" way before its time. Armed with $2,000, we planned out how to book a recording studio in town, do a recording session, *and* manufacture 200 cassettes!

The first step was choosing songs to record. I had garnered a lot of requests over my years at the piano bar, so it was easy to decide which songs to put on the first album: the most requested songs at the time. We called the album *By Request* (DUH!). To date, that album has sold over 650,000 units, and many of the songs on it continue to rate among the most streamed of the 365 songs that I have recorded over the years on 30 albums.

$2,000? Wait—What? So, How Did We Do This on Such a Tiny Budget?

Here's how. We hired the studio and engineer for one day; I recorded 16 songs *in that one day* and then still went to work that night at the dinner club. Specifically, I arrived at the studio at 9:00 a.m. on a Wednesday, worked with the engineer till we got the sound that we wanted (about two hours), then sat down to the freshly tuned piano and played nonstop for around seven hours. I recorded 16 songs that I had been playing nightly at the restaurant—*play, listen back, correct; play, listen back, correct, and so on.* We left the studio at 6:00 p.m. so I could go to work at the piano bar at 7:30 that evening. We had the record mastered by the same studio, and it was ready for manufacture in about a week. We then had to approve the master, decide on the order of tunes on the album, and give all that information to Judy to actually get the cassettes produced, a task for which she had been preparing herself from the time that we decided to do the project.

What? You Don't Have a Record Label?

Make your own! Judy created a record label called MagicMusic Productions and started out at once wearing all the hats that many people at a traditional recording company do for producing and releasing a record. At the time, that included arranging the entire recording process, from booking the recording studio to renting a piano, working out the details of the *how* of creating a cassette—including the acquisition of mechanical licenses for our cover tunes—finding out how and where to manufacture the cassettes, designing the layout and artwork, writing copy and credits, getting the whole lot to a manufacturing company, and managing everything else necessary for getting the product out the door to the distributor. Incidentally, manufacturers normally have an art department if you need help with the packaging or templates for their print requirements if you're good with design software. All very doable but someone has to actually *do* it!

About a month later we had a release party at the dinner club, where we gave out the 200 cassettes to our wonderful patrons and so paid back the "loan," and that started the ball rolling.

Okay. You have an album. Now what was that marketing strategy?

1990: The Gift-Shop Market

In the early '90s, there was a brand-new business model called "in store, play, and sell," in which the music of only a few artists (normally fewer than 10) was being offered for sale at the checkout counter. That was important. It was a very astute marketing strategy. Music of some kind has always been played in retail establishments to set a mood or create a pleasant aural backdrop for the shoppers. At that time, the music was usually furnished through traditional radio stations or subscription services. The difference in the new model was that the shop played music over their sound system throughout the day *in order to promote that particular music to their shoppers.* If a patron liked the music, she would walk up to the counter and naturally ask, "What is that playing?" The CD would be for sale *right there at the counter.*

Because we now had a product that could be played and offered for sale in gift shops that were implementing that marketing model, Judy did extensive detective work through *Billboard* publications and others to find out which distributors were handling that niche market. She then sent our cassette to *all of them* that were promoting my type of music. At the time, there were eight (out of literally hundreds that she researched) that seemed appropriate. One distributor responded. We contacted them. Individual stores usually ordered maybe five units at a time at the beginning, so in the first month, that distributor asked for a paltry 30 cassettes. But the orders increased very swiftly because there were literally *thousands* of small, independent gift shops across the country that used this model, many of which became outlets for my music.

We were still handling all the upfront expenses of manufacturing the cassettes to deliver to the distributor. After a few months, they needed more than we (at our own expense) could produce. We couldn't get a bank loan based on the *hope* that we could sell a lot of cassettes. So, we partnered with the distributor, and they took over manufacture and packaging. It turned out to be quite a successful model for us. By the end of year one, we had sold around 30,000 cassettes and were on our way to making a living with recorded music. However, although the album sales were doing very well, I kept my "day job" playing cocktail at the dinner club for another two years, not taking any chances.

The gift shops turned out to be a perfect outlet for my music. The people who frequented them tended to belong to the demographic who generally liked the type of music that I (and others like me) were playing. So we found ourselves, quite by chance, in the *gift* industry rather than the music industry. Remember this because this is important—*you don't have to take the normal route that everyone is taking.* We got into the record industry through the side door.

We were an independent when that was fairly rare in the industry. And although we were never mentioned in *Billboard*—being "off the radar" in a sense, as we were mainly successful in the gift marketplace—we had annual sales upwards of 350,000 units in each of several years and were, according to music industry standards, in the top 5 percent of sales in the record industry as a whole at that time. Also, by those standards, the aforementioned album, *By Request,* achieved gold record status, having exceeded 500,000 units over a period of a few years. Yet we had started our journey on a cocktail pianist's salary and little experience in the recording industry.

In other words, *you* can do it too!

My CDs also occasionally found their way into the traditional record chains, like Tower Records, Sam Goody, and Camelot, but they were normally relegated to the scary, kiss-of-death easy listening section at the back of the store collecting dust, as the shoppers in those stores were mostly teens and young adults looking for the latest chart toppers. But the music sales in numerous gift stores across the country got my name out and about, so that by the time I was ready to do my first solo concert, we already had a good deal of national name recognition.

1991: The Road to Playing in Performing Arts Centers

One day, while I was still playing at the dinner club and my first album was up and running, I said, "You know, Judy, I would love to do an actual concert in an *actual* concert hall," in other words, not in a restaurant or club.

What do you suppose I did about it?

That's right—nothing.

What do you suppose Judy did?

She read some more books, learned the basics of concert promotion, networked with people in the local area, rented a beautiful space at the performing arts center in town (one that had a concert grand piano), scheduled the piano tuner, and set up a concert for me. In other words, we were self-presenting my first professional concert, i.e., paying the upfront expenses and then selling tickets, hoping to break even. By now, the healthy sales of my music (still cassettes at that time) provided the revenue to cover those expenses.

Promotion, printing of tickets, press releases, and advertising to make sure you have an audience—all these things have to be thought out and need to happen on a timeline. To make any event happen, you need to promote it. To promote something, you need promotional *materials*. Performance venues will do all of this for you, but be aware they will charge for those services. Fortunately, Judy happens to be *very* artistic. Lucky me! She has created all of our promotional materials from the beginning, which has entailed setting up and managing photoshoots (hiring a photographer, choosing wardrobe, finding a space to shoot in, and so on), creating CD catalogues, brochures, one-sheets, programs, and other specialized pieces. How did she do that? She read books. She studied online. She learned on the job. She was already computer-savvy in programs like Excel, Quicken, and Word. Later on, when it became necessary, she taught herself Photoshop. She continued to educate herself in each new discipline as the need arose. Together, we produced my first concert performance.

Me? I just walked out onstage and looked pretty.

So, after that very first solo show, I said to myself, "*Well! That was easy!*"

I only found out much later that because I had a Judy, I was in the "FLC," the "Flippin' Lucky Club." Someone has to do all that (absolutely essential) stuff.

Now I had caught the bug and wanted to do more concerts. More work for me and more for Judy. In the beginning, most performances were fundraisers for causes we believed in, private events, and performances for nonprofit organizations of various kinds, often done gratis or with only expenses taken care of. A good way to get a start on becoming a performer on a concert stage is to offer your services without remuneration for a cause you truly wish to support. It is worthwhile. It creates goodwill, and most importantly, it feels wonderful to be able to help people and causes that you truly believe in. How lucky we are that we can raise large amounts of money by doing what we love!

This was the beginning of a very successful and long-lasting performance career. When you do a successful concert, word gets around. Concert bookings for nearby venues started coming in through word of mouth. However, this meant that, in addition to all the other hats Judy continued to wear, she had to become knowledgeable in writing contracts and technical riders, drawing stage plots, liaising with tech crews at the halls for sound and lights, and being the contact person throughout the planning process, often for many months leading up to the concert. In addition, she scheduled the piano tuner for a time when I could be there to see if anything needed handling; she booked hotels, and occasionally flights, and saw to it that everything happened on performance day that needed to happen. Eventually, we were doing as many as 30 concerts in a year, without an agency behind us, so there was a lot on her plate.

As the number of concert performances continued to grow, we networked with people in the music business whom we had known from our time in LA. We were very fortunate to reconnect with and learn from people like David Bretz, a former tour and production manager for jazz great Chick Corea. In time, he became my manager and took care of all those aspects of booking, touring, and performance tech that were still new to us. He made life on the road seamless and practical. David created our contracts in-house and saw to the technical side of things, while Judy took care of the record label. He also introduced us to the existence of various arts presenter organizations, the regional and national association members who book performing arts centers. With his guidance, the show grew so that we needed more help. At one time, we had a tech crew consisting of four people, an assistant to handle merchandise sales at the venues, and another wonderful person to look after our (young) kids when we were on the road. At the same time, Judy made the show look like a "show" and not a "recital." She did that by creating lighting cues and bringing stage dressing of various types including drapes, lighting accessories, and other stage set items.

I still depend on Judy to be my ears in the hall for sound check; she provides emotional support in the recording studio and at live concerts. She really wears all the hats of a record company, which is what we *are*, albeit a very small one. For several years, we were both label and distributor, and as the company grew, Judy eventually managed five employees for the label to enable us to handle the increased demand for my CDs. I had recorded 20 albums by that time, and we were doing all the manufacturing and shipping from our own recording studio.

This chapter is not written as an encomium for Judy, although she deserves one; this is a discussion of **what has to happen for a career in music to blossom**. It doesn't happen without someone doing all the heavy lifting in the invisible background.

On the Road

For these actual shows on the road, which, after all, were the *raisons d'etre* of all this work, we had a daily routine for each show. We arrived at the hall at 10 a.m. and worked through most of the day to put on the show at 8 p.m. For Christmas shows, in addition to our usual stage set, we brought 12 five-foot lit trees. During most of the day, Judy would be with the tech crew, dressing the stage, directing the final lighting focus, rehearsing sound cues, assisting with sound check, and building as many as 30 lighting cues. She made sure that I had everything I needed for the show and, in general, checked every detail (including the steaming of my stage clothes) so that I could play my best without any distractions. All this had to be done before 6 p.m. on the day of the show, so it was a busy day indeed.

After the show, I was busy meeting people in the lobby; our assistant was selling CDs, and that left Judy to pack up the mics, the drapes, the pedestal table, the water glass, and other bits and pieces that we may have brought with us and to make sure everything we loaded *in*, was actually loaded *out* when we left. Then, after load-out (which usually takes about an hour *after* visiting audience members), we tried to find a restaurant open at that hour—usually about 11:30 p.m.—before driving back to the hotel. Unfortunately, in most smaller towns that usually means Waffle House. We have a season ticket there. The next morning, we would drive—or fly—the several hours back home and prepare for the next show.

This is not meant to be a detailed record of our journey. Suffice it to say that we had to grow our career by ourselves **by figuring it out** (with a great deal of wonderful help), just not from an outside label. As the market topography changed, so did we. (Translate "we" as "Judy.") As I mentioned earlier, when digital streaming with iTunes was brand new, Judy got my music up and going soon after that service was available. Same with Pandora and Spotify. Once again, you keep your eyes and ears open and figure it out.

All that to let me just walk out onstage like I'm a rock star. I could not do it without a tremendous amount of ongoing support behind the scenes. *But you have to have a Judy making sure that all of that activity happens on a timeline.*

Regardless of how I may make fun of myself, I wasn't sitting idle all this time. Concerts in performing arts centers were new to me, and although I couldn't wait to get onstage and play, there were all sorts of preparations to make. Besides learning the repertoire, creating strong arrangements for each tune, programming the shows, and deciding what to wear onstage (*yes, even a guy has to decide what to wear and to make sure everything is taken to the cleaners between gigs*), I wanted to have humorous monologues in my show. So, I had to write them. I had to create and program a two-hour, one-man show that held people's interest and that incorporated my original humor into the introductions to the pieces or songs I was about to play. It's just the way I decided to do it. My six years of playing piano at the Comedy Store in Los Angeles certainly helped a great deal, but I had never written any comedy of my own. I had listened to—and *studied*—hundreds of comics and learned why some were funny and others crashed and burned onstage. I wanted to create some amusing monologues, and I needed help.

Judy to the rescue!

"Why don't you talk to your friend Mimi?"

Now why didn't I think of that?

One of Judy's most useful traits is that she connects the dots. I got in touch with my dear friend and stellar actress/singer/comedienne Mimi Wyche, who gave me some invaluable guidance and coached me through my first feeble attempts at that kind of writing. Together, we wrote my very first scripts. Since that time, Mimi and I have worked together in many shows at a local theater. Besides being a wonderful actress, she is a comic genius. She put me on track so that from that point forward, I had a starting place to write humorous monologues that I have continued to create for my show.

As time passed, I got some great writing help from another comedic wizard (and close friend) named James Sibley. Over the ensuing years, we tweaked the show, wrote a great deal of comedic material, changed the program about a hundred times, and continued to try to make it better each year. We have performed over 100 shows together.

After about 12 years of doing my show, I added a new ingredient—a brilliant vocalist, Dana Russell, who can sing just about everything, from rock to sultry ballads to musicals and light opera. She is a charismatic performer and adds a new, wonderful dimension to the show as a featured artist. She still performs with me today.

There were some other incredibly talented people with whom I connected in the performing arts area. Very early on, Allen and Suzanne McCalla, the artistic directors of our extraordinary local theater, the Greenville Theater (imagine that!), were very influential in my development as a performer and entertainer. They allowed me to put on my first show in their theater to try out my brand-new curtains, smoke, snow, and fog machines, magic devices and other stage props that I would have had no opportunity to use without their generosity and knowledge of stagecraft. Under their artistic direction, together we created and mounted rather extravagant Christmas shows, modestly called the "Greenville Theater Christmas Spectaculars," with a cast of 20–30 actors. We performed those shows throughout the Christmas season for six years in a row. In addition to those seasonal shows, I was still performing my solo piano show throughout the rest of the year. I continued develop my show, write new material, and let the show evolve. The reason I am relating all of this is to let you know that you don't get "there" on your own. So many people have helped along the way. If you're focused on your goal, you seek them out, or you "run into" them, seemingly by happy chance.

Booking Conferences

At some point in our evolution, we needed to attend regional booking conferences. As I said earlier, David Bretz introduced us to the existence of arts presenting organizations, in particular the Association of Performing Arts Presenters (APAP). This national organization has regional groups as well. Members include concert venue executives, booking agents, and artists. At the time, we were still independent, so since we didn't rely on an agent, we attended many of these conferences ourselves in order to get bookings.

However, as our business expanded, we also found that we needed artist representation to handle the increasingly busy schedule. At one of the conferences, we hooked up with our first agent and continued our forward progress because of the professional connections that we were able to nurture at these three-day events. There is much, much more, of course, but this is a synopsis of our journey.

Why am I telling you all this? **Because:**

Good news! This is all doable. You can do it too. *Your* way. But you need someone (even if it is yourself) to undertake all of these tasks and to build relationships in order to be artistically and financially successful over time. Today, that means understanding and using social media, new streaming platforms, and who knows what else that is coming down the pike. But you need to know—as early as possible—what it takes to put on a professional performance and create a successful career. It doesn't just "happen."

The good news is that tutorials on all of this stuff abound on the Internet, and you can start from anywhere. Have a question? Just Google it. And then, if it "feels" right, *actually do what they suggest*. (Hint: most people don't. So, if you do, you are already ahead of the game.)

I urge you to not take this lightly but to become aware as soon as you can of some of the numerous ingredients that go into making a career in music alongside the realization that *you can do it without a big organization behind you*. But you must educate yourself along the way and work things out so that you don't appear unprofessional, naïve, or just plain ignorant. Fortunately, nowadays there are unending *free* resources on every aspect of the music business available online. I encourage you to use them.

I think that we musicians often want only to play our instrument and write our original tunes and arrangements. We likely begrudge the time we have to spend at the computer setting up dates, researching microphones and sound equipment, learning how streaming works, and the like when we could be practicing.

I have some news for you; you have spent a lifetime perfecting your craft and art at the piano or other instrument. That is why you are so good at it. Now spend just a *10th* of that time learning everything you can about the business end of things so that you will have a vehicle to show the world your music. Sometimes I go for two weeks or more without touching the keyboard because I have to write scripts, answer my mail, write original tunes, keep my tunes up on streaming platforms, reprogram my existing show, learn about streaming concerts, write this book, and keep in touch with fans on Facebook, YouTube, and other social media. By doing all this other stuff, you are creating your career and, thereby, your future income. Be happy that you have the wherewithal to do it. And try to enjoy learning all this technology that allows you to do what you love most. Often, you may need to spend as much—or more—time on the business side of music, and getting your music marketed in every sort of way you can think of, as actually spending time with your instrument.

Take tender loving care of your business; try not to hate your computer, and by all means, get yourself a Judy! Or be one yourself! This application of business acumen, love, and sweat, unswervingly applied, will eventually reach critical mass and finally make it possible for you to forget about everything except the music on show day so that, relieved of that stress, you can stride confidently onto the stage and

play it like you mean it!

APPENDIX

Easy Listening: Elevator Music Taken to New Heights

Sorry, couldn't help myself there; it's fun to joke about easy listening music or cocktail piano *(a miniature piano with a straw and an umbrella in it)*.

Silly jokes aside, I do not wish to demean the value of easy listening music in any way. The fact is, I *did* make my living for many years playing easy listening, cocktail piano, dinner music, and the like and talking over my own music to the crowd at the piano bar. ***And I loved it!*** Easy listening music plays a big part in our aural environment. But it is the very opposite of what you want in a concert.

You play an "easy listening" style when you, as a professional musician, are hired to play *in the background* for a couple of hours for, say, a cocktail party or some event where people are mingling, talking, and enjoying activities other than the music. You are providing a genuine service by creating a backdrop that puts people at ease. When you are doing this, please remember that, that is your *job*. You are not "performing." People will probably *not* come up and talk with you; you may feel unnoticed. That's okay. They are not being impolite or rude. They are simply not supposed to be listening to you. They are just noticing what a lovely aural environment it is. There might also be a lovely window treatment, but they don't comment on that either.

When I was playing piano for parties and other events for many years, the more I heard people talking and laughing—the noisier it was—the more I felt like I was really doing my job. I loved it. I was creating a space for people to be comfortable in. No one wants *silence* as the backdrop to a party atmosphere. It's easier to talk, to break the ice, when there is already some sort of sound tapestry in the background. And it's more delightful and genuine when the music is being played live. You are there to make the atmosphere that much better by what you do—almost invisibly.

So, technically, what are the ingredients of easy listening? Why do we call it that? Well, it is because the music, purposely, *does not involve the listener*. It is "easy to listen to" because the musician has removed all those "play-it-like-you-mean-it" ingredients, as they should. It is meant for the background, and like the artwork or interior decoration in a hotel lobby, for example, it is not meant to grab your attention so that you stop what you are doing and pay attention to it. It is there to make the existing environment a more pleasant space in which to do whatever it is you are *really* there to do, unlike the art presented in a museum or gallery. Why am I spending so much time on this subject? Because many of the pianists and other instrumentalists whom I know get offended that "no one is listening." They are not supposed to. It is not a concert. You still play your best, just not your concert arrangements.

Muzak

Many musicians make their living creating beautiful backdrops for life's experiences, and thank goodness they do! We live our daily lives with music in the background, from the time we wake up in the morning till the time we say goodnight. We enjoy music at the grocery store, the shopping mall, the coffee shop, and department stores. If all of that music were attention-grabbing, we would never get anything done.

Muzak (one of the first "easy listening" services back in the '50s) was a master at that. The station played covers of tunes we all knew and recognized but with orchestral arrangements, different tempos, and so on that made the music "stand out" less, so it did not interfere with our daily activities.

Muzak knew that if you take the *emotional content* out of a performance, you are left with a comfortable aural backdrop, like a muted paint color on a wall. *(By the way, this is just my opinion, and I never heard this stated as policy by **Muzak**, or anyone else for that matter.)*

Easy listening is not a musical judgment, just a genre.

So, if you are playing easy listening music—just this once—***don't***

play it like you mean it.
Just play it!

Accompaniment: Mind if I Join You?

Part of my career over all these years has always involved accompanying vocalists or playing for actor-singer workshops, dancers, improv groups, or the occasional fiddle or guitar quartet or trio. I love accompanying singers, comping rhythms in a jazz trio, playing the score for musical stage productions, accompanying choirs, playing the gorgeous piano parts in classical art songs, and nearly any sort of joint venture where you, the pianist, are the necessary, important support for the music *but are not the featured artist.*

All you really need to know about accompanying well and properly is contained in that above statement. **You are not the star** in this case. If you want or *need* to be showcased, don't accompany another artist.

But if you do decide that you want to accompany someone, please be conscious of your role and play accordingly. That said, you are not in a subservient role. You are absolutely essential to a great performance. You are there to make the soloist look and sound her best! It is not a contest; it is not even a duet. It is laying a foundation for the soloist to soar above. She needs to be 100 percent confident that when she takes the next step, the pavement will be there holding her up.

I learned a great deal about accompanying in college when I had to play piano for vocal students, concert choirs, and student recitals. I learned how much a soloist depends on the music that carries him along like the river beneath a boat. You see the *boat*, but the water is the reason it can stay afloat. Always remember that. The soloist (let's just say "singer") is dependent upon you to sink or swim. Accompanying a fine singer is a highly skilled, *profoundly responsible* position. You can make or break the performance. On one occasion when I was accompanying a nervous student in recital, I realized during the performance that he would not be able to hold the note as long as needed, so I moved the accompaniment along faster underneath that particular phrase so he could get to the end of it and catch his breath. He thanked me later. But I knew what to do. Why? Because I **listened** to him. I knew that my role was to make him sound the very best that he could sound. If I did it right, no one would ever know that he was in trouble. He knew he could depend on me. And that is what your costarring role is: someone that can be depended upon to keep the ship afloat no matter what.

I think that is the most important understanding that a good accompanist has to grok. When the performance is over, the soloist will graciously acknowledge you; you take a modest bow, then look back to the soloist to help direct attention back to her, and follow her offstage. After the performance, everyone will flock to the soloist, as they should, and you can collect the music and disappear into the background or ride off into the sunset. Doesn't matter. You have done a great job. Sometimes being invisible means you did a great job. We say that the bridge is beautiful; we don't necessarily think of the massive structure that holds it up, hidden from sight.

Accompanying is a noble profession and one that I have loved and excelled at for most of my career because there are really two of me. One is the entertainer and star of my own show, and the other is the tasteful musician who plays in the background, enabling the singer to shine, soar, and receive their much-deserved accolades. What a joy!

Depending on lots of things, for example, whether you are hired for this one gig or are working with a fellow musician, friend, or cocreator, you will usually have to defer to the soloist's musical choices of tempo, dynamics, phrasing, and all the other performance decisions that occur within the music. After all, it's *their* show. Get really good at putting your musical tastes aside during that song, for that is also part of your job. And then truly commit to the "new" way of delivering the music so that the performance is as strong and sincere as possible.

You can also have a two-person "musical conversation" in some instances. Earlier I mentioned that I work on a regular basis with a truly fine vocalist named Dana Russell. She and I have performed together for years, so by now we know each other pretty well. When we embark on a new musical journey with a song we have never done before, we already know each other's tastes, so our joint project going forward from the get-go is smooth sailing. It is not a duet; mine is still a supporting role, but I can use more of my improvisatory skills to make the accompaniment more interesting without interfering with the "main event," so to speak. When you are working as a team, as we are, of course, everything is a musical conversation.

And speaking of "musical conversations," when you are playing a *duet*, or even an accompaniment, in the interlude, for example, it can occasionally be appropriate for you, the accompanist, to have a moment in the spotlight. I sometimes, with Dana, play an extended interlude in which I do not hold back but play as though I am playing a solo arrangement. That is a mutual decision and requires careful consideration of the musical end that you are trying to achieve. I only mention this because, like everything else, musical collaboration has no hard-and-fast rules. It must take its final form based on the experienced judgment and good taste of the players involved and conspire to make a statement that you both agree on.

So just remember your part in the play. If you always want to be in the spotlight, don't be an accompanist. If, on the other hand, you delight in helping to make another artist dazzle the audience, this is a rewarding way to do it. Then—*together*—you can

play it like you mean it.

Music for Hire: Playing Private Engagements

Many of us make our living by playing at the huge variety of private events that individuals and corporations host: weddings, birthdays, bar mitzvahs, Christmas parties—celebrations of all kinds.

Here are a few ideas for those gigs. Do your (extensive) research way ahead of time. Find out the age of the people you will be playing for. If it is a corporate event, find out what products they sell or endorse so that you won't step on any toes or make an unforgivable faux pas (like drinking a Coke at a Pepsi convention). In other words, do your homework and be flexible. Learn commercial jingles along the way; maybe learn to play the notes that a cell phone plays when it rings, things like that. Be creative and fun.

When you are playing for a dinner party, you ought to be in the *background*, so even if you are playing one of your "best" arrangements, just play it in a vanilla sort of way. You don't need to play the entire concert arrangement, just make it pleasant and recognizable because you are not trying to attract attention to yourself. You may think "Why did they even bother to ask me to play?" But **the audience is never wrong,** and it's *their* party, so you may just be like the flowers and the punch bowl, part of the scenery that, all together, create the ambiance for the evening. But remember that—for whatever reason—it is still YOU they wanted.

Depending on the environment, you may only need to play one-third of the song or do a much shorter arrangement of it. It's a job. It's "work for hire," which is a perfectly respectable ingredient in your professional career.

You still play sincerely and beautifully, but don't expect them to listen to you, and don't force yourself on them either. You may not even get to play *one* song in your "concert version," and that's OK. So, don't feel slighted if you do not have a chance to play the whole song and don't get angry at your host or employer if she asks you to take a break, play more quietly, or play through dinner. If you really hate it, then next time don't take that kind of job.

Speaking of which—let's say you are asked to play for someone's celebration, and you really don't want to, for whatever reason. I don't have a pat answer. However, you could say, "Thank you for thinking of me, but I just don't have the time to prepare and give you the performance you deserve. Here's a person you can try."

Or you could ask, "What kind of music do you really like? What about having a trio playing soft jazz?"

Or you could say, "My friend is a DJ. She sometimes does (wedding ceremonies). Since you already have a DJ at the reception, she could probably do the ceremony as well."

Piano Bar: Can We *Talk*?

What about playing cocktail piano at a piano bar? I did that for *many* years early on and absolutely *loved* it. I was very successful at it because I am naturally outgoing, and I love talking to people. It was, for me, like going to a party every night.

Playing piano bar requires a certain skillset—namely, the ability to *talk and play at the same time*. Also, if you are a fixture at that piano bar, then you need to learn your regular clients' names and their favorite songs and play them when they walk in. At one lovely dinner club where I played for about six years, six nights a week, I kept a card file handy and wrote down the names—and songs—of everyone I could remember from each evening. Many of them came in night after night, so it was easy to learn their names and songs. I noticed that I learned their favorite songs even before I was sure of their names. But as I said, I kept a file, and each night at home, I would add to it, look over the list, and commit some to memory, hoping I would see them the next night so I could play their song before they requested it.

I might put reminder notes in their card, like "great hair," "loud talker," "endearing smile," or "lots of hand gestures"—anything that struck me about them *that I could look up* in my card file alphabetically, in case I needed to remember the name that went with that "endearing smile" (under the letter *e* for "endearing"). I might write down "He has a deep, resonant singing voice," "She looks like that actress from Bewitched," and maybe what we talked about—hobbies, the school they went to—whatever it took to jog my memory. By the way, I still have that file, and by the end of about five years, it had around 1,200 names and tunes in it. I knew most of them. It wasn't a gimmick. I wasn't using a mnemonic device. It wasn't "muscle memory." I am not blessed with a great memory. The reason I could remember them was that I spoke with these people night after night and made some lasting friendships with great people, some of whom I still see on occasion, now 35 years later.

What I am emphasizing with this example is that there is a lot you need to do to be happy and successful in your career besides being able to play the piano beautifully. You will, of course, need to learn numerous songs appropriate to the age group you are playing for, but they don't all have to be wonderful or extensive arrangements. The thing about playing someone's favorite song is that they want to hear the "punchline" of the song, the hook, the recognizable part. So, make sure you know that part at least. Usually, people will be chitchatting during it anyway, as it is a party at the bar, and they are listening for the familiar part. That doesn't mean "cheat." Play the whole song if you can, but be aware that at some point—usually right after the recognizable, signature part of the song, they might stop listening altogether and get more involved in their ongoing, lively conversation. That is fine. You are not in Carnegie Hall. When that happens, and the talking really gets loud and lively, it's is a great sign that the "party" is going well. I normally back off, play more quietly, and be the wallpaper of the club at that moment.

In any party atmosphere, including—and *especially*—on cruise ships, people are primed to have a great time; they want to go home and tell their friends they had the *best* time listening to—and talking with—the *best* pianist! They *want* you to be great and are very forgiving; and they are delighted that you even know the song or gave it a try. People are wonderful around a cocktail bar. That's because most people are kind, fun-loving, and good to each other. The piano bar gives them (and you) a place to visit, see their friends, and catch up on news; it's a safe environment in which to meet new people and enjoy some good music. Think of what *you* like to do when you go to a bar, club, or restaurant. Well, that's what your clients want to do too. So, help do that for them. At the cocktail bar, it's not all about the music; it's about them, them, *them!*

So, if you are playing in, specifically, a piano bar where people are sitting around the piano or at tables near you, engaged in talking to each other *and to you, too,* well, then it requires that other ability I alluded to earlier (talking and playing at the same time).

Frankly, it may be a difficult skill to master, but it is one that is entirely necessary if you are going to play in restaurants or bars where you are featured but not "the show."

Here are a couple of little exercises I employed all those years ago to acquire that skill.

Exercise one

Sit at the piano and get ready to play a piece of music that you know inside out, one that you can play in your sleep (try a slow ballad at first). Now, place an open magazine or book on the music rack—preferably a page that has no pictures and thus is easy to read; it doesn't matter what it is about—

and start playing. While you are playing, begin reading the page in front of you **out loud**. At first, you will probably have difficulty reading anything at all, except a word or two, but after a while, you will get through a whole sentence without making any musical errors. As you get used to it, you will find that you can read a few sentences in a row. Very likely, you will find that you are reading words (or playing the song) in a jumpy, disjointed, or quasi-rhythmic sort of way without any real understanding or reading in a rhythm that coincides with what you are playing. However, as you persist, you will find that—at some point—your brain will begin to separate the two activities, as though they have nothing to do with one another (which they don't). You will soon be able to do the two disjunct things at the same time, and you will read with understanding and play the song musically at the same time.

Exercise two

The next step, of course, is talking to a real person in real time. When you are practicing at home, alone, or wherever you practice, try saying "Hi" into the air. Practice "Hello," then "Good to see you," or "I love what you've done with your hair!" to *someone who is not there* or to a sibling or parent, without stopping what you are playing. At first, you may find that you pause for a second or two, long enough to just say "Hi," and then continue playing. That's OK. Baby steps. You could ask someone a simple question, like "What's the weather like out there today?" and make sure you understand the answer.

Take it from there and make your own exercises, always improving your ability until you can carry on a simple conversation while not stopping what you are doing musically. "Bit by bit this tangled web ..." ***untangles!*** and you are comfortable doing both activities simultaneously. It's a fun "trick" to have in your repertoire, and one that attracts lots of attention, because it is obviously an unusual and difficult thing to do. In addition to bringing smiles, it will make you much more in demand at every venue you play.

APPENDICITIS: OOPS! I MEANT APPENDIX 2

(Yeah, there's *more*! I know! That's how it sometimes feels to wade this far into a nonfiction book.)

On the Road Again: Did You Remember to Pack a Toothbrush?

For those of you who will be traveling, doing a tour, even traveling to one concert and then home again, there is a lot to think about besides the music. Whenever I travel to play a concert, I bring a suitcase full of *things*. I hope you like *things* because you are going to need them. You never know what situation you are going to run into.

Every concert hall *ought* to have a dressing room with a full-length mirror and a place to hang your clothes, a green room, or a side stage—and a way to get to the stage from said dressing room. But that is not always the case. You would not believe what some *very nice halls* use as dressing rooms, how far away they are from the stage, and the accoutrements that are missing. So here are some tips on being as well prepared as possible for whatever comes up. Don't assume that everything you asked for will be there.

Here is a list of *things* I always take with me.

For the Dressing Room

Several clothing hooks that fit over the dressing room door. Remember that the door is probably **thicker** than the doors at your house, so look online for one that can handle a door that is two and a half inches wide, with extra hangers to hang your clothes on. They make some that are adjustable for different door widths. There should always be a garment rack, but sometimes there just isn't one. I believe in redundancy because I don't want any last-minute surprises.

Items to prevent clothing malfunctions! There are some famous ones! I don't want to be one of those! Do you? Soooo … I always bring an extra pair of shoes, shoe polish, and plenty of socks. A shoehorn, a lint roller, an extra belt, an extra shirt, extra ties, a hand towel. And a professional steamer for my clothes. I also bring a small travel iron.

Sewing kit. Mine has several needles (already threaded!) with heavy-duty black and white thread for shirt buttons, suit buttons (hence the heavy thread), and whatever else may come along. Of course, scissors, safety pins and straight pins, extra buttons (specifically for your onstage clothes), and whatever else you may think of for sewing emergencies. I also like to bring an eyeglass repair kit.

Hand mirror. In case there isn't one in the dressing room. Obviously, you can't travel with a full-length mirror, but always ask for one in the tech rider. That doesn't mean there will be one.

Shaving kit. Chapstick, hand lotion if you use it, nail clippers, file, hairbrush, comb, razor, touch-up makeup, deodorant, toothbrush, toothpaste, mouthwash, cough drops—in other words, **your shaving kit** (or cosmetic bag). And don't keep it with your regular stuff at home. Make a separate kit that always stays ready to go. Check it now and again to be sure you have everything in it that you may need.

Writing utensils. Pens, pencils, paper, note cards, and a notebook of scripts. I like having the chance to make notes about the current venue, write down names of people I should thank or acknowledge, this and that. More than one pair of reading glasses if you need them and a small pen-knife to open CDs with at the merch table later on. Those commercial CD openers never work right. With regard to pens, besides the normal ballpoints, I have a couple of gold and silver gel ones for autographs on dark posters and glossy paper, or CD jewel case inserts, and a few Sharp-ies—thick and thin—for everything else.

Load-In

Tools. It never hurts to have a few basic tools in your car. I keep assorted sizes of screwdrivers (flat-head and Phillips), a couple of pairs of pliers, a wire cutter, a small hammer, a hex wrench set, adjustable wrenches (a few sizes), a utility knife, and several pairs of work gloves, plus anything else that you may find in a basic tool kit.

Gaffer tape: black. NOT DUCT TAPE! As I have mentioned before, you do not want to be locked out of your dressing room! Depending on the venue and the maintenance crew, they may have a door to your dressing room that automatically locks after you leave. If I am not sure about that, I tape the latch and deadbolt in an open position. I do not want to get back to the dressing room at the intermission to find I cannot open the door and I cannot find the person with the key. Also, gaffer tape has a million uses. I bring Velcro for the same reason. Sticky-back and plain, always **black** in case it is for use onstage. I also bring a big, fat doorstop, big enough to hold a heavy door open. Many times, the doors are commercial ones that automatically close, and you may want it to stay open while you are bringing in your gear. Also bring a heavy-duty, 30-foot grounded extension cord (black).

Warm Gloves. I bring winter gloves (mine are leather with lamb's wool inside) even in summer because occasionally the sink has only cold water or lukewarm "hot" water, or the air conditioning is so cold that you freeze in the dressing room. You may think "What kind of halls is he playing in?"

but you would be surprised. Some really beautiful halls might have a temporarily nonfunctioning water heater or a crazy-cold air system that can't be adjusted locally and is cooling the entire house. I need my hands to stay warm up till the time I walk onstage. Many backstage areas just aren't as carefully maintained as the public spaces—understandably.

Artist bench repair kit. Rarely, but it has happened occasionally, the adjustable concert bench that comes with the (rental) piano is out of whack, or noisy, or uneven. I have an "artist bench repair kit." You can find one online, and you can therefore make the whole evening worry-free. In addition, I take along *(and use very often!)* those circular rubber, stick-on non-slip pads that fit on the feet of the bench. Often, the stage has a slick wood floor, and the bench can slide. The pads are removable and don't hurt the bench. So, unless you are Victor Borge, you really don't want to slide off the bench in the middle of the Hungarian Rhapsody. Include **WD-40** in your bag of tricks for obvious squeaky reasons.

Piano tuning hammer. I am *not* a tuner! But I always bring along a tuning hammer and two mutes in case there is one note that is out of tune and the piano tech is not available. I can usually tune *one* note! Umm … *usually.*

Onstage

Microphones. I bring my own (Countryman ear-set mic for speaking and also Earthworks mics for the piano), but that is not really necessary. Also, my vocalist's wireless microphone kit. If you are planning to use the house equipment, be sure to request what you need well in advance of the concert. And learn the brand and model numbers of the equipment you are bringing or requesting. Learn whether they require phantom power or not. The tech crews need to know that information. Even if you are using the mics furnished by the house, make sure to bring a mic clip that fits all sizes, just in case. I use the spring-loaded ones that fit small- to large-diameter microphones. I also bring a couple of microphone cords—long ones (25 feet), just in case. We also carry with us a drab black cloth that is cut to fit exactly on top of a concert grand piano lid. When the lid is up, as in most concerts, stage lights can bounce off the lid of the piano, reflect off the "cyc" (cyclorama—a cloth stretched tight along the back of the stage), and interfere with the lighting looks. We try to think of everything. I don't like surprises on show day.

Drinking glass. I bring a plexiglass water glass (plus an extra one) for use onstage. Plexiglass so that it won't break in transit and because, you may be surprised to hear, sometimes the venue can't find you a decent drinking glass for the evening. Because I don't like to drink from a water bottle on-stage, I bring an attractive *small* pedestal table for my water glass and notes, one that I can assemble and take apart without tools and fits in my suitcase. I position it upstage of the piano, so it is nearly invisible to the audience but handy to me when I need it.

Bar stool. My vocalist uses it for some songs. If you use one, bring it. They make great lightweight folding ones for a few dollars. Don't expect them to have one for you—or if they do, it might be in horrible condition.

Handkerchief, program, notes, or whatever you keep inside the piano. I always remove the music rack and place these items on the upper end of the harp or on the tuning pins. Don't wait till the concert to write out anything you need as a reference. Have a clean white starched handkerchief inside the piano where you can easily reach it and an extra hanky in your pants pocket or sport coat pocket. If you wear a suit or sport coat, you probably want a pocket silk and a spare (also freshly ironed and chosen carefully) and an extra tie or two if you wear one.

Load-Out

Have a LIST for load-out! Don't leave anything behind. You'd be surprised how easy it is to forget something because as you are in the lobby, meeting and greeting, the tech crew are putting away your mics, closing up the piano, and setting everything aside for you to load out. It is very easy to forget that you have a handkerchief in the piano. Or they might think that the water glass belonged to the theater, and so on. So **have a list.**

Immediately after the Concert, at the Hotel

Evaluate the concert: how you played, audience response, age group estimate, how many tickets were sold, how much product. Did your spoken words go down well? Do you need to change a punchline or alter your script in some way? How did your voice sound? Did the jokes work or fall flat? Try to remember any discomfort you may have felt and fix whatever caused it for the next show. Do it now before you forget, while it is still fresh in your mind.

Most importantly, how was the piano? Who tuned it? Did it stay in tune for the whole evening? Did you get his card or contact info at least? If he was great, you want to be able to use him again. If not, you may want to request a different tuner next time you come back to that venue. What brand and model of piano was it? Make notes about the piano to send to the venue afterward. For example, did you find that it needed voicing, regulating, or pedal adjustment? Anything that you might discover during a concert that wasn't part of general tuning and maintenance. The venue will thank you.

You are as ready as you can be for the next performance. With all of this nonsense taken care of before you head out to the next venue, you can be relaxed, comfortable, and single-minded about the performance.

Hope this helps.

EPILOGUE

When you walk out onto the stage, whether it be in a living room, a piano bar, a club, or a concert stage, you should feel a sense of ease about what you are about to do and a little twinge of excitement because you are about to give your audience a very special gift.

You want the outpouring of your mind's musical wanderings to flow unhindered into the ether, to make its pilgrimage to another's heart and mind; you want to invite your audience into your universe to share with you for this time *something*—a glimpse even—of how you view the world, how you feel about the beauty that surrounds you and that you are creating on the spot, the melodies and improvisations that give rise to joy or sadness or a host of other emotions at the piano. You are at peace and alert at the same time. All the hours and years you have spent at the piano, all the devices, techniques, physical and mental stress, intellectual challenges, all the considerations of difficulty, the effort, and the drudgery and hard work—all this history is disappearing as your fingers move from one succession of musical ideas and events to another—culminating in the poetry that is *you*! All of these disparate ingredients are finally coming together to dissolve into one unhampered musical utterance—notes, phrases, and emotions melting seamlessly into each other as you present one unified whole, a true gift of love, like one all-encompassing embrace.

Whenever you play,

play it like you mean it.

DON'T READ THIS PREFACE

It's for me. That's why I have put it at the end of the book. The editors felt it was too long or boring. And no one reads prefaces anyway.

So, close the book and don't read this preface.

PREFACE

> "…That my whole life is a song, there is nothing in me that is not also music. Ah! my Heart! and Oh! my Song! where are you leading me now?"

I wrote those words in my journal one rainy day in the practice room at Baylor University, where I was working on my bachelor's degree in music performance. Those words, that question, rhetorical and actual, still resonate today all those years later.

At the time I wrote them, I was working on Chopin's majestic *G Minor Ballade* and had just reluctantly got up from five or six hours at the piano, the usual daily practice session for all music majors. I vividly remember that I felt on top of the world, utterly energized, excited, enchanted, empowered, elated, ecstatic, ebullient, and lots of other emotions that start with *e* that I can't name at the moment but that express themselves so very readily through music. It is still as alive in my memory as it was in reality, all those years ago. It's my "happy place," an illogical synthesis of *outrageous joy and untroubled peace* at the very same moment. I can go there any time I like. I can recreate that happiness and express it to others through music.

I am incredibly fortunate in that I have had the piano as a constant companion throughout my entire life. I can sit by myself on a rainy day (or a sunny one) and let my heart and mind flow through my fingertips and into the world. I have this one glorious outlet for everything I love, everything I believe, through the language of music.

But not just that.

I love to make people smile, laugh, and maybe even cry by playing music that moves them and brings back cherished memories. I want to help them remember their dreams and goals, the loves of their lives, the happy times, and occasionally the very sad times too. In a holistic sense, music reminds us of the precious, wonderful emotions that let us know with intensity that we are vitally alive. We feel it in every cell, every pore of our bodies and souls, that feeling that only music can bring us.

I have been playing concerts in performing arts centers for about 30 years, in every sort of environment, on phenomenally beautiful instruments, and, sadly, on occasional pieces of junk. I have performed in gorgeous concert halls and dilapidated barns. The one ingredient that is constant, regardless of the environment or the instrument that I am playing, is that I am able to connect emotionally with the people who listen to what I have to say musically. Naturally, everyone is happier, and there is a better shared experience in a palatial hall with a magnificent concert grand piano, but that is not what makes an outstanding performance. The most compelling ingredient that makes the difference between a skillful performance and a memorable one is the musician's ability to project emotion across a distance. In this volume, I have offered my musical and philosophical approach to playing the piano in the hope that you, too, can cross that spiritual divide and share your personal musical gift with your listeners.

Good luck and happy playing!

I told you not to read this preface.
The End
It's Finally Over

MUSICAL INDEX

ACKNOWLEDGEMENTS

A book doesn't suddenly spring into existence without the help and support of some very remarkable people. For me, this book is a sort of synopsis of a lifetime of experience, support, and learning from so many outstanding people–a wonderful journey that I owe to the numerous people who have made an indelible imprint on my musical, intellectual, and philosophical life, as well as having encouraged and nurtured my natural bent for playing piano. It would be impossible to thank them all, so I apologize in advance if I have left you out. Everyone who has touched my personal/professional life has contributed to my becoming a better performer and entertainer.

First of all, I wish to express my genuine indebtedness and gratitude to my entire family. I was born into a home that loved and revered classical music and the fine arts. Eureka! Lucky me! So the first obvious acknowledgement goes, quite genuinely and directly, to my parents, **Emil and Anne**, and to my three sisters, **Emilie**, **Pam**, **and Barbara**, who have been musical companions throughout my childhood and on till today.

To my three extraordinarily gifted daughters, **Lahren**, **Elizabeth**, and **Kristin**, thank you for putting up with my pursuing a crazy schedule that so often kept me away from home and interfered with any kind of "normal" schedule you may have hoped for. I am proud to be your dad, and I thank you for the inspiration and reason to pursue what is my life's purpose. You made it easy for me to be me.

And I just loved my grandma! Thank you, **Grandma Pandolfi** for your truly inspirational words of encouragement from the very beginning.

To wit:

Grandma (first generation Sicilian-American), to my four-year-old self:

"What do you want to do when you grow up, caro Emiliano?

Me: *"I want to play the piano."*

Grandma: *"That's-a nize-eh, my big-eh big-eh boy!"*

You couldn't ask for a more enthusiastic endorsement than that!

And since hers–and all our families'–were Italian-American households, you can imagine there was no shortage of emotional outpouring on a daily basis. That unrestrained expression of *"this-is-how-I-feel-about-this"* has had a marked effect on how I play the piano–then, and now.

Outside of the homestead, I received ongoing instruction and support under the expert supervision of my truly gifted piano teachers: **Wesley True, David Gibson, and Thomas Redcay**. Way beyond just teaching me how to play the piano, they became family friends, philosophical mentors, and "pals" during my years in high school and in college. I always had someone to talk to when I needed to work out personal or intellectual conundrums, or resolve a syncopated rhythm in my life or music.

My heartfelt appreciation goes to **Bill and Sibyl Thomas**, both fine musicians and great teachers, who, in my formative years introduced me and our family to the musical elite of Greenville, SC, where I grew up. With their guidance, our family became very deeply involved with just about everyone who was part of the musical life of our town and the state. They were our first introduction to real-live professional musicians, and we now all knew for sure that that was what we wanted to do for the next 40 years or so.

To my dear friend and extraordinary acting coach, **Robert Hanley,** I express sincere gratitude. The very many hours I spent as an accompanist in his class watching him bring out the best in his students was of inestimable value to me! Seeing him direct scenes, work with students and nurture their innate talent has rounded out my musical education from an *acting* viewpoint and made me a more complete performer. I learned from him how to "be" onstage.

When I first moved to Greenville, SC I needed a place to play. To **Vince Perone**, and the Perone family, I owe my thanks for providing the finest restaurant/piano bar a cocktail pianist could ever want: an elegant, fine restaurant with a baby grand piano with a glass lid that doubled as a bar. The **City Club** introduced me to so very many outstanding and influential people in Greenville, SC where we still live. I always remember those years with a smile.

I owe a huge debt of thanks to my first commercial music distributor, **Lifedance Distribution**, headed up by **Morris McClellan**, exceptional classical guitarist, **Lewis Ross**, and his wife and CEO of the organization, **Eleanor Ross**. It was they who provided my first foray into the alternative music market and ushered us into the world of turning recorded music into a viable career.

An enormous thank you to my dear friend and kindred spirit, **Deven Stross**, who managed the distribution of my first many albums at **Consensus Management**, and became our business advisor and consultant to my wife, Judy, who was heading our fledgling business back in the '90s. He continues to be my dear friend and unofficial personal therapist when I need to understand my career path or life direction more clearly. I couldn't do without him.

I have recorded thirty albums (first on reel, then cassette, then CD)–25 of them with my friend and expert recordist, **Kevin Nettleingham** (Nettle-ingham Audio) in Vancouver, WA. Kevin knows how to capture the most dulcet, bell-like pianissimos, and crashing fortissimos on a Steinway con-cert grand. He can make the recorded sound both thrilling and pleasing to listen to. *It ain't as easy as it looks!* I love working with Kevin. His slogan for his studio is "You, only better". I love it.

I mentioned **David Bretz** in the book, but I want to also thank him here for the inestimable value that he brought to our company in those years that we were lucky enough to work together. Besides educating us in the on-the-road routine, he is gifted at dealing with people on the road and at home. Great friend, great tour manager.

James Sibley is one of the funniest people I have ever known. He and I have worked together in more than a hundred shows, and his contribution of belly-laugh humor and personality caricature brought my show to a new level. It is largely because of him that I learned to how to create a comical version of myself on stage. Thank you, my friend.

Mimi Wyche is a longtime friend, one of the most talented people I have ever met. As an actress, she moves you to laughter or tears; as a singer, her operatic voice is powerful or delicate as the music demands. As a comedienne she has the audience doubled over with laughter. I credit her with starting me on the path to writing comedic monologues and putting together my first solo show.

Stephen Barefoot, my booking agent for many years, I owe him a huge debt of gratitude for making North Carolina my second (professional) home. Way beyond his being a terrific agent, he is a funny, entertaining guy to be around. *"Everybody loves Raymond"*? No! Everybody loves ***Stephen!***

To **Dana Russell**, world-class vocalist (everything from pop to light opera) and—more importantly—world-class friend, thank you for being so much more than a musical companion on stage. Her voice is enchanting and her charisma on stage is undeniable. Through our mutual love of beautiful music we have become more than friends—extended family. I love making music with you, Dana.

A heartfelt thank you! to **Barbara King**, a true friend and world-class travel professional. Because of her experience, expertise in her field, and her desire to introduce my music to a broader audience, she has made it possible for me to perform in St Mark's Square in Venice, the Catherine Winter Palace in St Petersburg, and numerous other European venues that will take your breath away. *(Apparently, she knows everyone in the world on a first name basis)* Thank you, Barbara!

Very importantly, I could not have done without the ongoing help from our "Gal Friday", **Kelley King,** who for so many years was our office manager, event-planner, CD sales supervisor, sometime baby-sitter, kid wrangler, the friendly voice on the phone, and anything else that was needed to make MagicMusic run smoothly and uninterrupted when we were in town or away. When you needed anything done now, urgently, after hours, any time, she was always there. Thank you, Kelley! For being part of our family.

I would particularly like to express my heartfelt thanks to **Suzy Gallamore Jewell,** another indispensable person who shared our personal and professional lives as the children were growing up. We were on the road for over 100 days a year for several years, often with the kids in tow. We couldn't have handled that schedule without Suzy to look after the kids on the road trips, keep the home fires burning, seeing to the kids' schedules, and taking care of all the essential comings and goings that are part of a busy life in and out of town. What a gem!

To the brilliantly talented actor, singer, coach, dear friend, **Doug Shaffer,** who—all those years ago (in the '90s)—orchestrated my first "big" show, replete with stage dressing, costumes, curtains, lights, special effects and magic elements, so that my show evolved from a concert into an actual "show", a genuine thank you.

Now that I had this "big show", I needed a place to mount it.

Enter **Allen** and **Suzanne McCalla.**

It would take several pages to adequately acknowledge **Allen** and **Suzanne McCalla**, artistic directors of the Greenville Theater, for everything they have done for me and my career. They have supported me professionally and personally, on and off stage for around 25 years. Because of their gen-erous permission to use the theater over many years, I have been able to develop and refine my own show, experimenting with magic effects, having a large cast of talented people to work with, and honing my own skills as an entertainer under their guidance, in addition to being musical direc-tor for their truly entertaining, over-the-top-produced Christmas shows. I learned so very much about stagecraft, set design, artistic direction, re-hearsal routines and the like from working with them. Thank you, **Allen** and **Suzanne**, for everything.

My deepest continuing gratitude goes to **Julian Doyle.** What can one say? A lot of what I know about marketing my music has come from him. Having spent a lifetime in marketing, he is the person who got me to really understand that music is a business. Besides being a dear friend and coun-selor, and producer of my album of musicals with the City of Prague Phil-harmonic Orchestra, he has tutored me in some of the aspects of business that I never learned along the way. I hope that you have someone in your life who can do that for you. Thank you–both **Julian** and **Liz!**

To **Gayle Winston** and **John Stewart,** two extraordinary, one-of-a-kind (two-of-a-kind?) people that you read about in 19th century novels, well-read, scintillating personalities that you hope to meet one day. I have been that fortunate. Gayle the entrepreneur, chef, Broadway producer in her former life, is proprietor of the River House, a unique country inn nestled in the mountains of North Carolina.

Through Gayle, we met **John Stewart**. I miss John, the most remarkably intelligent, yet down-to-earth person I have ever met. The author of thir-ty reference books, he seemingly remembered everything he ever read or wrote. He was the most fascinating dinner guest one could imagine.

Throughout your life–if you are lucky, you meet some extraordinary, unique individuals who–just in a personal, indefinable way, contribute to the quality of your life. My very special British friends, **John** and **Jane Harvey** are two of the most remarkable people that life has sent my way.

John and Jane arranged for me to perform in the heartbreakingly gorgeous! Liverpool Cathedral, one of the highlights of my performing career.

To my dear friend and wordsmith, **John Pendley**, I want to offer my special thanks for the in-depth discussions and candid reviews of my piano arrangements that he has given me over the years. His broad knowledge and understanding of music combined with his astute observations have shed a spotlight on musical elements in my playing that I do instinctively, but that I may not have specifically named. Those discussions have helped me to verbalize some of what I have to say to students in this book.

David Cook, dear, dear friend, music lover and pianist, we truly miss you. Thank you for introducing me to some extraordinary classical music that had somehow escaped my radar over the years. Some of the pieces that you brought to my attention are now part of my performance repertoire. Again, David and his remarkable wife, **Charlotte Cole** have become a special part of our lives forever. We are fortunate indeed, to know you both.

Oh my! **Verna Puntigan!** Poet Laureate of South Carolina (a recognition that she has earned in several different years) Verna, your "Playing Pianissimo" has such a personal, quietly emotional passion in it. That poem is what made us friends all those years ago. I visit it often, for the heartfelt beauty that it brings. It is delicious to read. Thank you for the beauty that is in your heart and in your words.

James (Jay) Fallon. What can I say? This man is the most versatile genius I have ever had the privilege to call friend. In addition to being a multi-platinum engineer, and producer, he has an 18 year study at The Juilliard School in composition, conducting, and piano performance and is and editor of over 7 Juilliard School textbooks. Beyond his musical accomplishments, he is an Airline Transport Pilot; he holds advanced degrees in physics, electrical engineering, and computer science with over 250 patents issued and pending in the fields of aerospace, computer science and medicine. the founder of Ithaco Space Systems and Realtime Data. His abilities and encouragement have helped me to push the limits of what I think I can do.

Thank you, Jay, my friend.

Last—and most, it goes without saying that my wife, **Judy**, has been my rock and grounding point all these years. Without her holding the reins, I would gallop off into uncharted territory, just playing any ol' music, willy-nilly, without a path or plan.

She knows I know that.

The End.

Aug. 29th
2015

To Emile,

I dedicate this following poem to you. This poem appeared in the book "Golden Words" in 2013. This poem won me the title "Senior Poet Laureate of South Carolina of 2013"

"Playing Pianissimo"

It does not mean silence, like the absence of the moon in the day sky. It doesn't mean barely to speak in the way of a chaos whisper.

To play pianissimo is to carry sweet words to a lonely woman in the last row of a concert venue who cannot hear anything else and to lay them across her lap like a cape.

Warmest Regards,

Verne L. Puntigan

Thank you for the beautiful music. Your gift brings to all who are fortunate enough to hear your CD's or hear you in concert.

Here's what they're saying about...

EMILE PANDOLFI

THE CRITICS:

"It is rare indeed to hear a pianist who plays with such passion and grace. Unprecedented in its teaching, Emile shares with us his unique approach to pianism that has traditionally only been handed down from Master to Apprentice. A must read for pianists young and old!"

—James Fallon, multiplatinum engineer, producer and composer, editor of over 7 textbooks at The Juilliard School.

"Pandolfi joined the orchestra to play Gershwin's "Rhapsody in Blue" with rhythmic precision, secure finger technique, verve and convincingly strong articulation. He added fun and excitement to this already jazzy classical piece and the audience responded with enthusiasm. Following this, Pandolfi had the stage to himself. He is a very...theatrical and musical performer...a medley of sparkling Disney tunes was facile...; the audience loved it...Pandolfi has a talent for humorous quips and for being able to guide his audience from listening to popular tunes to enjoying music of a classical nature."

—C. St. John, The News & Observer, Raleigh, NC

"I want to thank you personally and on behalf of the symphony, also, for your super, super playing. It was indeed outstanding and brilliant, to say the least...I have done the Gershwin several times, but have never heard it played more expressively...the audience really responded well to your personality and playing after the Gershwin. I think that they could have stayed all night. It was certainly one of our most successful concerts...It was a great pleasure for me to work with someone so professional and talented!"

—Alan Nielson, conductor of the Raleigh Symphony Orchestra, Raleigh, NC

"No matter what they're calling it, the soothing sound of Emile Pandolfi on the piano has equaled national success."

—Nicole Pensiero, The Press of Atlantic City, Atlantic City, NJ

"Pandolfi's solid piano technique gives him the freedom to interpret music with sensitivity and delicious abandon. Thundering octaves, shimmering trills and runs,...oh, so infectious...Pandolfi has a relaxed personality and comic repartee of an entertainer."

—Nancy R. Ping-Robbins, The News & Observer, Raleigh, NC

"He (Emile Pandolfi) plays standards from Broadway, Tin Pan Alley and Hollywood in a free-flowing manner that seems to go the music's very soul."

—Robert Deutsch, Stereophile Magazine (under "Records to Die For")

"Attending his performance is comparable to having friends over to enjoy a national recording artist in your living room."

—Sherry Williamson, The Cary News, Cary, NC

PRESENTERS:

"Once again, on behalf of the staff at the PAC, I want to thank you for the opportunity to present your world class production in our theater. It is the high water mark for this theater's five year operation!"

—Richard Ludwig, Manager
Performing Arts Center, Middle Township, NJ

"Wow! Such natural talent, humor and stage presence. You so totally endear yourself to your audience. And does the audience ever appreciate you and have fun! It was a beautiful production."

—Joye Burkhardt, Event Chair, Family
Counseling Center (fundraiser), Greenville, SC

HIS FANS:

"...The magic of ...your performances never cease to amaze me."

—Nick A. Theodore, Lt. Governor, South Carolina

"I think you play beautiful...I hope someday, I will be that good. I am only 10 and I'm taking piano lessons from my old teacher...I would love to hear you play in person one day."

—Carmen Lyn S., Sierra Vista, AZ

"As I listen to your music, I smile, cry, laugh, remember childhood images, sounds and ripened passion. Your music provides the glue that holds together both past and emerging memories...so, you see, your music touches many lives in ways that you may never know. But then, that is the magic of giving what you love."

—G. B., Farmington, NM

"Our lives are enriched for having your alive, inspiring, pleasing and wholly entrancing music...you bring sunshine into a lot of lives. Words cannot express our gratitude."

—Mrs. T. R., Middleville, MI

...ON THE OTHER, *OTHER* HAND...

"I've heard worse."
Grampa Pandolfi

Oh...yeah, he's OK, I guess…"
Some guy.

On being asked, 'So, how did you like Emile's latest album?' the late, great, **Liberace** once said, "Who?"

"He still owes me three dollars!"
Bob F, college roommate

"It was loud enough".
Morris McClellan, on hearing Emile's rendition of "Malaguena'

"A little too enthusiastic for my taste."
Emile's meditation instructor.

"His mewsic is jes great to **rock** by!"
Mizris BJ Cooter, 95 year-old stunt-rocking-chair champion.

"Emil haas tza potential off bekommink ein trooly inconseqvential pianeest!"
Herr Dr. Ich-bin-ein-Muzic-hasser, Direktor, Klavierinstitut von Heiligenstadt

For more, *actual* information about Emile, make sure you visit his website at *www.emilepandolfi.com*

THANK YOU FOR YOUR PURCHASE

and read of *Play It Like You Mean It*.
Reaching readers like you is
exactly why I wrote it.

Did you like this book? I would love to hear your thoughts on it.

What's next? Consider leaving a review! You can leave a review on Goodreads or on the book's product page on the retailer's website where you purchased this book.

Also consider sharing your thoughts about the book on your own Facebook or Twitter, and feel free to tag me!

Don't miss the latest updates and more at www.emilepandolfi.com, and let's continue the discussion!

Listen to the *Play It Like You Mean It* playlist on YouTube by scanning the QR code below. Listen to my arrangement of each song listed in the book. Enjoy!

WORKS CITED

Bonpensiere, Luigi. *New Pathways to Piano Technique: A Study of the Relations Between Mind and Body with Special Reference to Piano Playing*. Philosophical Library. 1953.

Fothergill, Alastair. *Planet Earth*. BBC Natural History Unit. 660 mins. 2006.

Jones, David, dir. *84 Charing Cross Road*. Columbia Pictures. 1987. 100 mins.

Krasilovsky, William M. and Sidney Shemel. *This Business of Music: the Definitive Guide to the Music Industry*. Billboard Books. 2000.

Yeats, William Butler. "He Wishes for the Cloths of Heaven," from *The Wind Among the Reeds*. Elkin Matthews. 1899.

CPSIA information can be obtained
at www.ICGtesting.com
Printed in the USA
JSHW022115120322
23709JS00001B/3